C000146940

# TREALES, WHARLES & ROSEACRE

# "RECOLLECTIONS"

*written & compiled by*

## JENNIFER ROBINSON & JOE LEE

### in collaboration with the people of the parish

Landy Publishing
2000

© The compilers claim copyright in the text of this book. Landy
Publishing asserts the rights of copyright..
The terms of the Copyright, Designs & Patents Act, 1988 and the
Duration of Copyright & Rights in Performances Regulations, 1995, are
to be applied.

ISBN 1 872895 52 2

British Library in Cataloguing Publication Data.
A catalogue record of this book is available from the British Library.

Layout by Mike Clarke, 01254 395848
Printed by Nayler the Printer Ltd., Accrington, 01254 234247

Landy Publishing have also published:

*Lancashire, this, that an't other* by Doris Snape
*Lancashire Lingo Lines* dialect poetry edited by Bob Dobson
*Blackburn Tram Rides* by Jim Halsall
*Accrington's Public Transport 1886-1986* by Robert Rush
*Clitheroe Ablaze with Glory* by Sue Holden
*Lancashire Bonds: Poems and Monologues* by Alan and Les Bond
*Wrigley's Writings* by Bernard Wrigley
*Sand Grown: the Story of Lytham St Annes* by Kathleen Eyre

A full list is available from:

Landy Publishing
'Acorns' 3 Staining Rise, Staining, Blackpool, FY3 0BU
Tel/Fax: 01253 895678

# CONTENTS

Bill and Irene Robinson driving sheep near Manor House Farm, Church Road, Treales, 1995.

# INTRODUCTION

The idea for a history of Treales, Wharles and Roseacre grew from a suggestion submitted to the Millennium Committee as one way in which our parish could mark the year 2000. It was soon evident, however, that to write an academic account of the area would take years of research, so new parameters were set making this a relatively minor work - but one which might inspire future generations to extend. The Millennium Committee has tried to involve everyone in the parish in compiling these pages of memory and the response has been one of enthusiasm and co-operation. For this reason they would see the book as a *Millennium miscellany* of facts relating to those whose personalities have influenced our villages since the earliest times. It has always been the committee's intent to name all those resident in the community in the Millennium Year and should your name be missing from these pages it is by accident rather than neglect. It is hoped that you will enjoy this first attempt to catalogue the buildings, events and incidents that have touched those, living and dead, who have given so much to make this a fascinating parish. Perhaps anyone reading these accounts in the year 3000 will find them equally fascinating.

Celebrations held at New Year 2000 marked the start of the third millennium for this ancient parish, whose settlements existed in the first millennium and possibly earlier still. We therefore pause to reflect on what has passed in our own lives, and in the lives of those before us, who have made this parish what it is today.

Many ways of marking the occasion have been devised. A calendar was produced for 1999 showing old pictures of people and places in the parish. So great was the interest that a historical exhibition was held in the church in April 2000. Many, many people contributed and participated by providing and setting up displays of over 200 old photographs, many items of clothing, dozens of domestic artefacts, and agricultural implements. The exhibition was attended by over 300 people and was most successful in being both interesting and enjoyable for all concerned.

Whilst not wishing to live in the past, with its dangers of early death, and fear of poverty, we do recognise the rich heritage left to us. What pictures cannot show is the closeness of a community which had to be self reliant and supportive of its members. To a remarkable degree this spirit lives on in our parish.

Changes which occasion some regret are the loss of so many of the old cottages. Too frequently nowadays we have to protest when developers persist in bulldozing old cottages to build new suburban style housing. It has happened here very recently. We are trying to foster a greater respect for what we have inherited. Progress must mean improvement, not destruction of the old just for the novelty of the new. This community does wish to progress, but with sympathy for our inheritance moulded by past generations.

It is in this vein that the Millennium Committee has tried to operate. We built our first 'four poster' stone flower bed on Christmas Eve 1999 in Wharles and others are following in each of the villages together with other planting under the aegis of *'Fylde in Bloom'*.

Earlier this year every child in the parish up to the age of 16 was presented with a millennium mug designed by Chloe Hind, a pupil of Treales School.

The church bell tower was repaired and its bell refurbished and rehung thanks to the generosity and ingenuity of Marshall Towers and Ralph Huggett, in time for Frank Walker to ring in the new millennium.

In July 2000 we celebrated the Parish Field Day for the first time for many years.

All of these efforts have been supported and funded entirely by the people of this small parish of some 350 souls who have raised nearly £3000 without resource to council tax precepts or lottery funding. It is a source of pride that the parish of Treales, Roseacre and Wharles continues to be self reliant and as supportive as ever.

David Webster, Chairman.

Lord & Lady Derby at the reception given for them by the Fylde Estate Tenants Association when the estate was sold to the Church Commissioners for England. John Melling is in the foreground, Mr. Hale, Land Agent for many years holds a walking stick.

# TREALES, ROSEACRE AND WHARLES

### THE FIRST MILLENIUM

It is difficult for the layman to visualise what it was like to live in Northern England before and during the Roman occupation in the early years of the Millennium coinciding with the life of Christ. However, we can take comfort from the fact that historians and archaeologists also find it difficult. Investigation has shown that much of the settlement in those early days would have been in the vicinity of higher ground rather than in the heavily wooded and often, as in the case of Fylde, marshy plains and valleys. To give some indication of timescale it is known that by AD 70 the anti Roman faction in the Brigantes kingdom in Yorkshire overcame the pro-Roman Queen Cartimandua, which revolt initiated the establishment of a Roman legion at York in AD 71. Thus the Roman stranglehold in the North began in the early days of the governership of Julius Agricola around AD 74. The central factor in the history of the North under the Romans, is the overwhelming economic and social impact of a large and well paid army whose occupation relied on a network of forts and roads. There is ample evidence that the parish would have been well known to the Romans being so close to one of their main highways. Work carried out in the 1950s and 1960s at Carr Hill, Kirkham, confirmed that there had been a Roman Fort there. A further excavation in 1994 by Lancaster University revealed ramparts of this fort. This structure would have been reached from the East along the well documented Roman road from Ribchester which passed through Fulwood (Preston) Lea and Lund and which was described in mediaeval manuscripts as 'Magnam Stratam' and 'Whattelingestrete'. Evidence exists that this road did link with the Carr Hill fort but whether this road continued further west along 'Danes Pad' is a subject of great debate. It is sufficient for us to know that the Carr Hill fort existed and overlooked our parish and that commercial intercourse would have occurred between the army and the scattered populations of the time. Those wishing to know more about Danes Pad, are directed to the Blackpool & Fylde Historical Society's 'Danes Pad – a Roman Road to Nowhere' by Ted Lightbown.

### Post Roman to Norman

Little is known of the area following the withdrawal of the Romans and the onset of what is commonly known as the 'Dark Ages', but we have chronological perspective in terms of the introduction of Christianity to these shores and its progression to the Norman Conquest in 1066. It is in the Norman Domesday Book that we find *Treueles* first described and recorded, listed as containing two carucates of arable land. Following the conquest, documentary evidence exists (9 John (1207-8)) that (the now spelt) *Trevles* was given to 'Robert de Vavassor, father of Matilda, widow of Theobold Walter'. Evidence also exists that Trevles, and other places, was in the possession of the Countess of Ormond in 1351 (Lansdowne Manuscript, 25 Edward III, 1351).

### Restoration (1660) to the Present Day

We know that subsequently Treales passed to the Butler family, but Croston in his History of Lancashire recounts that 'William George Richard, ninth Earl of Derby, in 1673, married Elizabeth Butler, first daughter of Thomas Lord Ossory, and acquired the greatest part of this district, and for him a manor court is held annually at Treales or Trayles the day before the court at Weeton'. Thus commenced an unbroken association with the Earls of Derby until the estate was sold to the Church Commissioners for England in October 1955. In 1971 the Church Commissioners sold the estate to the Pension Fund Property Unit Trust, who in turn sold it in 1987 to the Investment company Mountleigh. By the early 1990s Mountleigh was in some financial difficulty and the estate was broken up. Many farms passed to the sitting tenants but fairly large tracts of land were retained and sold to another company, Metacre, the first time in over three hundred years that the estate had ceased to exit as a single entity. The parish today consists of some 4000+ acres with a population usually around 350 to 400 adults. The parish is bisected by the M55 motorway; otherwise the boundaries and road structure have changed little since the area was surveyed for ordnance purposes in 1848. The Tythe Map of Treales, Wharles and Roseacre is held by the Lancashire County Archivist. Drawn by Chas Birket it is dated 1840.

### Origins of Treales, Wharles and Roseacre as Placenames

For more detailed information regarding the naming of our three villages we are indebted to one of our own parishioners, Christine Manton, who researched the area in her thesis 'A Place - Name Study of Kirkham and its Environs', presented in 1992. In her fascinating study she reveals the origins and variations in spelling of our village names. It has already been stated that Domesday Book recorded Treueles in 1086 and this spelling continued, appearing in four different historic documents until 1228. In 1242 the spelling was *Turuel* (Lancashire Inquests Part 1, Vol.XLVIII) and this spelling was preferred until 1249 when two different versions appeared in other documents, *Trivel* and *Treueles* as in Domesday. Various other documentary evidence between 1249 and 1637 gave *Trevell*, *Treweles*, *Treuelez*, until in the *'Ducalus Lancastriae Calendarium'* 1637, the present spelling Treales is met for the first time. Notwithstanding, the fluctuations in spelling continued from 1665, *Trayles*, 1671/2, *Treyles* (Registers of St. Michael's on Wyre 1659-1707) but even within the St. Michael's Church Register the spelling varied with different entries, *Trauler*, *Traueller* occurring on different pages. However, in the late 1600s and early 1700s the spelling as it is today seems to be standard. Both elements of the word Treales are derived from the Welsh/Celtic: *'tref'* - a farmstead, homestead, hamlet. This first element is found frequently in Welsh place names. The second element *'llys'* is also ('llys' - a court or hall) found in the Welsh, the two elements combining to form *'Township of the Court'*.

Christine Manton goes on to describe that *'names indicating true British habitative names from buildings are rare'*, and suggests that this is probably the only example to be found in Lancashire.

The earliest reference to Wharles occurs in the Lancashire Charter of 1225 and is given as *Parles* but this is thought to be a mistake on the part of the scribe, who could have mistaken or misread the first letter either Q or W. The name *Quarlous* appears in the Lancashire Inquests of 1249 and *Wherlows* in 1279 in the ledger of Vale Royal. Other spellings occur in other documents, *Warlawes*, *Wharlas*, until Wharles appears in 1672 in the pages of the Clifton Muniments. The registers of St. Michael's-on-Wyre are consistent from 1685 giving the present day representation. Again both elements of the name appear to have been from British stems, this time in old English, *'hwerfel* - circle, and *hlaw* - a hill or mound'. Combined, these elements give *'hill with a stone circle'*.

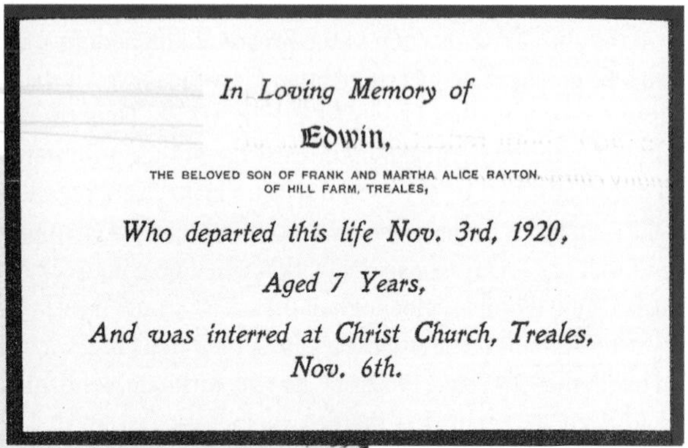

In Loving Memory of

**Edwin,**

THE BELOVED SON OF FRANK AND MARTHA ALICE RAYTON, OF HILL FARM, TREALES,

Who departed this life Nov. 3rd, 1920,

Aged 7 Years,

And was interred at Christ Church, Treales, Nov. 6th.

*Derby Arms*, Treales, with Melbourne House in the background. It was near here that Edward Rayton, aged seven years, was killed by a horse, November 3rd 1920, aged 7 years.

Work done by archaeologists suggests that where the Anglo-Saxon *hlaw* occurs in a place name this could refer to both natural and man-made hills and could refer to a tumulus (ancient burial mound). As the land at Wharles is flat then it is more likely that the tumulus theory could be correct and that there could have been a raised burial mound at Wharles.

The third element in our Parish was first recorded in the Lancashire Inquests (Part 1. Vol.1) of 1249 and appeared as *Rasaker*. Various different spellings occur from 1279 *Rosakyr*, *Raysaker*, *Rozaker* (1605) to Roseacre in 1633. In the St. Michael's registers the following entries are found between 1676 and 1695, *Rossiker*, *Roshker*, and *Rossacre*.

It seems agreed that in this case the name is influenced by the Norse '*akr*' and the Old English '*accr*', both reflecting '*a piece of marginally cultivated land of limited extent*'.

When combined with the first element, old Norse '*hreysi*', a cairn or heap of stones, Roseacre is seen as '*a field with a cairn*', a far cry from the idyllic picture that someone might conjure up today, 'a village strewn about with roses'. The author of the Oxford Dictionary of English Place Names, Eilert Ekwall, suggests that as cairns were often used to make boundaries, this links Roseacre to the stone circle at Wharles. Importantly Christine Manton hypothesises that the pronunciation of our village names evolved from the *original spellings* and has *not* been influenced by spelling changes through time.

### Strangers Hill, Wharles

Strangers Hill, is NNW of Locking Stoops, Wharles, close to the parish border. The name is of ancient origin and is so called because this was the spot where strangers who came into the parish and died would be buried. They were buried in this lonely place because it was not known who they were, what their habits were (they could have been vagrants or malefactors) or what their religion may have been. Therefore they could not be buried in consecrated ground. These unfortunate souls now rest in Strangers Hill. There are no records of remains being found at this site, nor if the site is related to the barrow or stone circle after which Wharles is named.

Rose Cottage, Treales, demolished 1960s.

### TREALES VILLAGE REMEMBERED
#### *A conversation with Grace Baxter*

We sat for most of a very wet February afternoon in the kitchen of Southview Farm, where Grace has lived since her birth in 1919. She insisted that her recollections of the village were not all her own but cumulative through the remembered conversations with her parents, grandparents, aunts and uncles and other village folk. One could sense everyday history as memory tumbled upon memory as her active and agile brain conjured the visions of yesteryear from her subconscious. Handicapped with arthritic knees she might be, but her mind is as lively as ever, her eighty years of experience translated into exciting word/pictures. Robert, her husband, sat with us, chipping in with snippets of fascinating details, which would be the catalyst of another burst of memory from Grace. I thought then of those gone whose combined memory and wisdom have slipped with them into eternity, without being recorded; how, had their recollections been recorded for posterity, we would have been writing not of fusty dates and buildings but of life itself. The interaction of village folk with their environment, their skills, achievements, sorrows and joys, now sadly never to be shared.

We started with a trip down the village street, her gaze through the kitchen window falling on Derby Farm which is immediately opposite South View. It must be nearly forty years since Derby Farm was worked by the Cooksons, but Grace remembered the Swans before Cooksons and then further back to the Butlers. She explained about Nellie Butler in graphic detail and told how most of the farms, strung sequentially throughout the length of the village street, were much smaller than they are today, a croft and two or three fields each. Old maps of the village show that this is true. The distance between Derby Farm and Hill Farm, (now Hill House at the corner of Spen Lane) is only fifty yards, yet Hill Farm, Grace said, was a larger farm than Derby Farm. Hill House must have triggered another memory, for then she was telling of the small boy, she couldn't remember his name, (but she had his mourning card upstairs), who had been killed, kicked by a foal outside the Derby Arms, going on to say that 'mourning cards' were common in earlier days, to be kept and treasured, a reminder of those who had formed the community, even though in this case the life was tragically short.

She then went on to discuss *the laundry*, the small cottage (now a private residence) adjacent to the barn on the westerly side of South View, telling of the Derby family and Mowbreck Hall and how Fred Crane (who worked at South View) would collect the washing from the Hall, bring it back to the laundry where it would be washed, starched and ironed, and returned to the Hall again.

The half-timbered houses recently occupied by a succession of gamekeepers and the Rawstrones, were comparatively new she said, being built in the garden of an old cottage, which like most properties in the village had a thatch roof. The Derby Arms evoked strong memories. Early in the century this was a much smaller, rural property, and Grace and other children, as they walked home from school, would watch Mr Swift, the then licensee, milking his one or two cows. The Derby car park, she remembered as the most beautiful garden, full of fruit trees, a superb white lilac tree, a vegetable plot fit for a king. Jimmy Lingard who gardened for the Swifts was very proud of his soil, she said - and then we were onto a different tack - Swifts Meadow, one of three fields rented by the Derby Arms, two in Church Road on the right and this opposite the Mill Field down the *'new road'* towards Treales Mill. She then explained that her aunts always referred to Treales Road (from Middleton Cottage to Treales Garage) as the *'new road'* because that was what it was. It had only been constructed in the mid-Eighteen hundreds - the original road ran down Moss Lane West, along the now public footpath linking Moss Lane with Treales Windmill, down the road leading to the mill and Windmill Farm, through the fields to Cardwells Farm and then on to Salwick and beyond. Something else she remembers about Jack Swift of the Derby Arms was that he was famous for his 'Hot-Pot' which he would distribute to the beaters on Lord Derby's shooting days, taking this in large containers on a donkey cart. She recalled that the 'gentry' would have their lunch at Treales Cottage, served by Mrs Kenyon and her husband, the Head Gamekeeper. Mr Kenyon, she said was a *"real gentleman"*.

Conversation inevitably drifted to Ash Cottage, recently demolished to make way for the new development opposite the Derby Arms, because this property was once the 'tied' cottage to their farm. Both she and Robert had been sad to see it go, not just because of the association, but because it too had been another of the small farms to line the village street. She could remember with

*"Ash Cottage ~*
*Treales*

Karen Baugh

Ash Cottage, Treales, demolished 1990s. Commemorative illustration by Karen Baugh.

Rural Treales. Spen Lane with cows.

Harry and Betty Hall buying ice cream
at the shop in Treales circa 1935.

clarity the shippon with a standing for six cows and the adjoining small barn with its beautifully crafted sliding panels in the walls in front of the cow stalls, through which hay could be fed to individual animals straight from the 'mough' (pronounced *moo*). She thought that the destruction of Ash Cottage was symptomatic of a modern disregard for the past, and had the cottage been theirs, they could have sold it a hundred times to enquirers eager to live in a property of some character - but then she was away again telling of the extension to Ash Cottage known as *'Sunny Nook'*, and then of Bill Cottam and his tobacco shop, which was also the unlikely source of parched peas which Billy made and sold to the village.

Of course the council houses in the centre of the village were newcomers, the site in the early part of the last century another thatched cottage and its croft, and opposite The Fold, down which was the cottage where Grace's father had been born. She told of the Tomlinsons of Stanley Farm, further towards Kirkham and still existing as a house, and Rawstrone & Hewitsons had also been a small farm with its own thatched cottage, tenanted by either Wilkinsons or Gornalls, she wasn't quite sure. She was more sure when she returned her thoughts to Ted Tomlinson however, remembering that he had a meadow down Moss Lane West, next to Butts Wood. It was then that both she and Robert deliberated on the fact that rented fields in those days seemed to bear no relationship with the farms and were often quite a distance away.

Continuing her verbal journey down the south side of the village street she described in detail the other small farms that made up the western end, Johnsons Farm and their Treales Smithy, where the horses were taken to be shod by Jack Johnson; then on to Primrose Farm, worked by the Willacys. Robert chipped in here to say that the same Mr. Willacy had once worked for Robert's grandfather, and finally to Whitehall Farm, sadly no longer a farm, its buildings to be converted, the home of the Coopers and before them the Milners. She then described the cluster of cottages opposite Whitehall and the remaining dwellings going back towards Church Road, all clearly remembered as if it were yesterday, even though they no longer exist.

It seemed then that she had exhausted her fund of stories till she suddenly retrieved a rather battered and obviously well thumbed story book from the cupboard alongside the cooker. She explained that this had featured largely in the reading matter not only of her immediate siblings and herself but also of her daughters and grandaughters and contained material that she thought should be taught to children today. She proudly announced that the book had been a School Prize, the inscription reading: *To Thomas Parkinson - Treales School 1888*. The title of the book was '*The Prize for Girls & Boys*' and was a bound compendium of monthly magazines, twelve in the volume, each monthly edition costing a penny.

Asked about her forebears she admitted that she didn't remember her paternal grandparents but remembered her mother's parents well. Her mother, Maria Crane of South View Cottage in Treales Road was the daughter of Thomas Crane, one of six children of whom one was to die in infancy. Her grandfather was a railway linesman responsible for the track between Salwick Station, along the Treales Roads to Kirkham Station. Grace recalled that she had inherited her grandfather's inscribed 'retirement watch' but had unfortunately lost it to an unscrupulous watch repairer, who later denied knowledge of having it in his possession. Life at the Cranes was a difficult if happy one. The house had no running water and no sanitation, other than an earth closet. Water had to be brought from a water pump along the footpath from Moss Lane West to Church Road by Bolton Houses, alongside Butts Wood, the pump emptying into a low trough which both Robert and Grace thought might still be there. This has been restored to mark the Millennium. Water for washing was gathered from a pit behind the house and then heated over the fire in a large iron kettle which hung from chains. Any baths the family had were taken in a tin bath in front of the fire.

Grace was one of three children born to Thomas and Maria Parkinson; Jack who was to farm Southview in partnership with Grace on her father's death, and Gertrude who married into the Benson family of butchers from Kirkham. Her father worked as a stable boy for the influential family of Claytons, Master Butchers of Preston, and who lived at Moorfield Farm, Treales Road. He was later employed by Lord Derby in the Estate tile sheds until offered the tenancy of South View Farm by Lord Derby in July of 1903. Grace remembers him with great affection, an upright, honest and hard working man, who had a lifetime passion for heavy horses. He bred Shires, and Grace remembers his favourite, '*Parkin*', bred from a farm mare by a led stallion (stallions were walked in hand from farm to farm for stud purposes) named '*Eddlington Blend*'. Parkin, she recalled won many prizes including a major prize at Shrewsbury Show. Apparently her father was very patient when breaking young horses to harness and one of his specialities was to train a horse to remain motionless should a heavy cart be upturned. We both recalled with great pleasure the last surviving South View heavy horse, Tommy, white and standing over seventeen hands, who spent most of his retirement in the Mill fields alongside Treales Road and who had a succession of friends who called daily in motor cars or on foot to spoil him. He lived to a very old age into the late 1960s.

She recalled that the family have always prided themselves in turning out good-looking cattle, although it was only comparatively late that the farm went over to Friesians. In the early days they had a small herd of up to fifty Shorthorns and Shorthorn Cross cows some of which were bought in from Ireland, imported via Preston and Heysham. When I asked how they transported cattle in the early days, both Grace and Robert remember walking cattle over fairly long distances. Robert, whose family farmed in Lea, remembers vividly walking cattle to Preston Market and Grace could recall cows being herded from the Freckleton dealer, Tommy Garlick's yard to Treales. She also remembers the cattle market in Kirkham.

The main product of the farm in the early days was cheese and she spoke with enthusiasm of the taste and texture of this home made product which was marketed in the Preston Cheese Market. She obviously enjoyed the weekly ritual of taking the cheese to market by horse drawn lorry, for she described the highly painted blue cart with red and white lettering denoting the farm name painted on the boarding. It was each Friday night that this special cart was strewn with straw, covered first with clean white linen cloths and the cheese placed in position. These were covered with white cloth and then again in inclement weather with a clean tarpaulin.

Jack Cooper at The Smithy, Wharles, around 1960.

The journey to Preston was a long and tedious one by heavy horse and she told how the horse would be left in underground stables in Lune Street in Preston, to be fed and rested before the return journey at the end of a long day. She particularly remembers one gelding Shire called 'Star' performing this weekly trip.

She then recalled her mother's role on the farm and in the bringing up of three children, but said that before being married her mother, along with many of the young school leavers of the parish had worked as weavers in the Kirkham mills. Robert described graphically the Kirkham skyline with seven massive mill chimneys visible from Treales.

She remembered many stories about her brother, Jack, and his empathy with his cows, and told of one dealer from Skipton who said that he had never seen anyone handle a large herd of cows in transit along roads from field to farm, as could Jack. This would bear out what is written in another section of this book regarding Jack's handling of cows.

It was getting perilously close to tea-time when we decided to call it a day, but not before Grace had escorted me over what seemed to be every square yard of land they had farmed. She knew the favourite places where the milk cows would graze, slight hills in shelter and sunshine where they would lie contented. She could identify areas of pure water and areas where specific wild flowers grew on the farm. She spoke of harvest and haytime and then produced the large earthenware jug (of which she has three) stamped 'Mrs Crane', which had been used by these early crofters to bring beer from the Derby to those working in the fields. She had given a fascinating insight into farming life, but I left, convinced that only the surface had been scratched.

Robert Baxter died on May 13th 2000, aged 81 years.

## WHARLES REMEMBERED
### A conversation with George Barnes

We met at nine o'clock on a Sunday morning early in March at Wharles Smithy. True to form George had been there for over two hours, Sunday morning is quieter and he can concentrate on his paper work. He was sitting at his desk with an attractive hen perched on the bench to his right side. He explained that this was the hen's usual habit and he gently lifted it down to make a little more room for both of us.

George apologised in advance for his memory, as though forgetfulness was an insult rather than inevitability as one gets older. True he couldn't remember the dates when the farm and smithy (it had been both) was owned by the Coopers, followed by Albert Rayton, but he surmised that his grandfather, Fred Barnes, had taken over the tenancy in the 1880s. Fred hailed from Derbyshire but moved to the Smithy from Cross House Farm, Great Eccleston. George explained that he had once had his complete family tree, but this precious document had disappeared one day from the Smithy, much to his dismay. His father succeeded to the tenancy around

1920. He explained that there had been a white thatched cottage attached to the end of the present brick buildings where they had all lived, the main road passing the front door and then sweeping to the left towards New Hall Farm. Typically this was a small, forty acre farm, supporting cows, pigs and poultry, as well as the Smithy.

His father was a renowned horseman and sought after by many owners to shoe their horses. He said that his father rode a cycle to most places in the Fylde, carrying horseshoes and his tools with him. He once tried driving a van but could not be persuaded to leave first gear, saying that it was fast enough for him. He quickly reverted to his bike and never mastered the petrol engine. George remembers him being responsible for the Blackpool Circus ponies and for many of the show-jumpers belonging to the once well known Harvey Smith. Smith would send a car for Mr. Barnes and take him to his premises beyond Clitheroe. He was also said to be in demand when horses were lame. It is common knowledge that a good farrier was worth his weight in gold with lameness caused by bad hoof problems, an area which often defeated the veterinary surgeon. He was always sought after to make shoes for show horses, fashioning bevelled shoes which would give the foot the appearance of being larger - was it Surtees who put the words 'No foot, no Hoss' into the mouth of his character Jorrocks?

George refused to follow his father with horses, concentrating rather on the automotive aspect of farming when it was his turn to run the Smithy. This was the era, the forties and fifties, when the tractor superseded the horse. He described the simplicity of the early Fordson tractors, easy to work on and reliable, and the innovative grey Ferguson, the first small tractor to exploit hydraulics. This revolutionised farming and much of George's early work was converting horse drawn farming implements to hydraulic/tractor use. He himself had worked for Isaac Ball for a little while before he took on the responsibility for the Smithy.

He recalled the *new road* (which left the Smithy in its present cul-de-sac) being built at the onset of war from 1939 together with the billets for Navy personnel which adjoined the road. These he said were beautifully kept with the most floriferous gardens. Five gardeners were employed to keep this area to its high horticultural standards and he remembers the superb rose beds alongside the accommodation.

Being young he was fascinated that the Fleet Air Arm ran the camp (nearer towards Inskip) as an aircraft carrier-aptly named *HMS Nightjar*. Here they practised landing and take off procedures as if from an aircraft carrier with first Fairy Swordfish marine aircraft, followed later by the Barracuda and Avenger planes. Here he paused and told how as boys he and his Wharles friends had often played pranks on the service personnel.

He said that they once put slates on the stove-pipe chimneys of the huts and then went on to tell how they put tin-tacks embedded in cow manure on the latch handles of the billet doors. The unsuspecting Fleet Air Arm personnel would prick their thumbs on pressing down the latch! He didn't elaborate what happened when the victim sucked the pin prick of blood from that thumb. He supposed that boys would be boys, although they were sometimes caught and soundly punished for their misdeeds.

He also remembered going with his father to Isaac Ball's 'shed' (as he called it) and being whacked soundly by old Isaac with a two-foot steel ruler, (the folding type carried by most tradesmen in a special narrow pocket in the leg of their overalls.) With tears in his eyes he asked Isaac what he had done to deserve that, *"It's not what you've done, but what you might do"* was the reply – not a very satisfactory answer for a small boy in considerable pain.

He remembered the Ball enterprise very well; the thrashing machines powered by steam which were later eclipsed by the Ford tractors; the road rollers which went as far afield as the Lake District and Yorkshire. When thrashing machines went out of fashion he remembered the combined harvesters and the other aspects of the Ball empire, crop spraying and then into the tarmacadam laying industry. Of course the work that this yard created for the Barnes Smithy was considerable, continuing under John and Victor Ball until David Douglas took over the yard and sought planning permission for houses. He wondered why the development couldn't have retained the name of 'Ball's Yard', a much more fitting name that the fanciful names conjured up by the developers and which would have linked this site with village history?

Although only a small village in the early days George remembered New Hall Farm when occupied by the Massams, and Jack Nuttall, and Boundary Farm with residents Bobby Swarbrick, who went to Inskip to a larger property, and Teddy Cooper. He spoke of Fred Alcock who farmed the *'Eagle and Child'*, and then of the locals whose pub this was. He reminisced about the Derby years and the policy of starting young farmers in the croft-type small farms, moving them to larger units when vacancies occurred. He then discussed the village under the Church Commissioners and of Colin Ralphs who as Major Brett's second in command at the Estate Office in Church Road (Major Brett lived in Halsall) gave orders to the Smithy for steel work and various other fabrications for the Church's estates, in Treales, at Chipping, and Halsall.

He also remembered the estate workers based at the Estate Office and Yard (now Carrsfield Barn) Dick Danson, Frank Walker, Jimmy Eccleston, Bob Bennett, Jim Dagger and Harry Hall. Walker, Eccleston, Danson, Bennett and Dagger were responsible for the upkeep of estate land mainly, while

Harry, joiner, spent much of his time at base. To work with the *'outdoor gang'* was hilarious, and worthy of a novel in its own right. He remembered several 'incidents' worthy of recounting, like the day Dagger, Danson, Walker and Eccleston, watched a dog eating Bennett's lunch without telling him, and the day that Dagger wrecked the Church Commissioners Estate vehicle. George said that the Estate had just bought a brand new Morris 1000 pickup wagon with a canvas back, which was used by the group to travel around the estate. On this particular occasion they had been called to a tree at Weeton which was leaning dangerously. Dagger said that he would soon cut it down – and did, right across the Morris 1000!

Rural Roseacre circa 1900

George often went with them to Halsall, near Ormskirk, which was then Headquarters of the Church Commissioners, Major Brett, the Land Agent living at Halsall Hall, an imposing Georgian house standing in a considerable estate. He was having trouble with rabbits destroying his beautiful garden and George was called upon to produce steel posts which would support wire netting – to be rabbit proofed by placing it sufficiently deep in the ground. He went as usual with the Treales workers in the now repaired Morris Station Wagon and was busy with them erecting the rabbit proof fence when Mrs. Brett came into the garden and said that the lavatory in the hall's cloakroom was blocked, and could something be done about it? Dagger, ever a gentleman said not to worry, he would soon fix it for her! Here George paused to say that the entrance to Halsall Hall was very imposing with a large and opulent hallway with the cloakroom leading directly from it through a polished mahogany door. Dagger, collecting the draining rods from the van, decided to fit the rubber plunger and rather than tackling the job from the cloakroom decided to back-rod from the manhole on the outside of the house. All went well until, as George said, Dagger came upon an obstruction and with a massive heave managed to clear the blockage. The next minute a very distressed and upset Mrs. Brett rushed from the house shouting, *"STOP, DAGGER"*, announcing that Dagger had filled the cloakroom and half the entrance hall with sewage. This caused great hilarity on the way home and Dagger was constantly reminded of this day for many years afterwards.

He remembered other characters with equal clarity – Mrs Blackburn who he said owned property all over, including Liverpool, and would take her cycle on the train to Liverpool to collect the rents. He remembers her as very good-natured. Her husband, who was the gravedigger at Treales Church, used to chew black twist tobacco which he would cut with his pocketknife into chewable pieces. He also mentioned Tom Rossall who used to call regularly at the Smithy, especially if it was raining, when he might stay for most of the day!

George's memory was functioning on all cylinders and I had to bring him back to our original topic – Wharles. His overriding impression now, he said, was that where as a boy and a young man everyone knew everyone else, today he hardly knows anyone in Wharles, and this saddens him. This must have sparked some happy memory of his childhood for he concluded our chat with a story of his mother who would always have his breakfast waiting for him when he had finished the morning work on the farm. He said that he could still smell the home cured bacon or ham, often served with fresh watercress that his mother had collected in the brook behind the Smithy. He said that her turnips, made in a large pot, cooked with butter and served with carrots and brawn or potted pork was something to remember - and so we both went our separate ways to lunch. The hen, that had listened patiently to our conversation from its perch went with him.

## ROSEACRE REVISITED
### A morning with Marshall Towers

We met on the morning of Maundy Thursday, April 20th 2000, this the first day of arguably the most important four days in the Christian calendar, a busy time for Marshall as he is currently one of the Church Wardens at Christ Church, Treales. He had kindly sorted out his recollection of Roseacre over the previous weeks, but he modestly declared that his memory didn't extend as far back as many of the other residents of the Parish, even though he has lived here all his life and is now in the early years of his retirement.

We mulled over our initial thoughts regarding Roseacre as we walked round the garden, both agreeing that of the three villages making up our Parish, Roseacre had perhaps the most appealing profile in terms of its compactness and true English village appearance, its buildings, old and new marrying well; it looks, we thought, as if it had developed organically (as the finest examples of England's villages have) rather than been the figment of a beaurocratic planning mind. Later, as we sat more comfortably round the fire, he was to remind me of the fine avenue of elm trees which once added to the beauty of the village street, but sadly these had succumbed to 'Ceratocystis Ulmi', the fungus responsible for the demise of this most English of landscape trees. His recollections of course went beyond their sheer beauty to more practical and expedient manoeuvring of tall loads of hay through the tunnel created by the upper branches of the elms. This he said was often fraught with danger and one could easily lose the top, if not the whole load, should the vehicle veer too close to the tree canopy.

He established the fact that he had, before retiring to Roseacre Cottage, his present home, had the tenancy of Derby Lodge Farm, Roseacre, which he had tenanted and bought after the death of his father, (also Marshall) who had worked the holding with his wife, Mary. His father had been brought up at Bradkirk Hall Farm, on the Kirkham to Weeton Road and had married Mary Walton of Staining before moving to Derby Lodge. He remembered that before the Towers, the holding had been in the hands of the Rawlinsons, the Eccles and before them the Heskeths.

In his lifetime at least two village farmhouses and two cottages had disappeared from Roseacre, he said, being particularly acerbic regarding the Church Commissioners. He said that if a property was old in the sixties, the Church couldn't wait to knock it down and replace it, as they had done with Post Farm, and Roseacre Farm, now the home of the Noads. He recalled in particular the old Post Farmhouse, of ancient wattle and daub construction, once thatched, but then roofed with tin, which despite its great age and historic interest had been systematically purged by the Commissioners. I was able to sympathise with him here, remembering the superb barn and outbuildings which once graced Windmill Farm on Treales Road but which were inexplicably demolished by the Commissioners, leaving the next tenants of the house with no garage or workshops, nor the potential to keep stock or horses, not to mention the total lack of shelter the buildings provided from the cold East winds. Marshall remembered the interior of Post Farmhouse with great clarity; stone flagged large kitchen sporting a massive fireplace with an unusual first floor gallery, accessed via a staircase, on three sides with rooms opening off it. He hasn't seen anything like it before or since, and felt the destruction of such buildings was an affront to our heritage. Roseacre has its fair share of modern housing which has fitted into the pattern of the village, but he still feels that to deny prospective villagers the chance to live in a truly historic dwelling was symptomatic of the thinking in the 1960s and indeed into the present day, remembering the loss of Ash

Cissy Salthouse of Woodbine Cottage, Roseacre, circa 1918. Note the carbide cycle lamp.

Woodbine Cottage, Roseacre, home of the Salthouse family, seen about 1900.

Cottage opposite the Derby Arms. He was lucky he thought to live in Roseacre Cottage, once tied to its parent farm, Roseacre farm, and home of the legendary Sam Salthouse, of whom he was to speak at greater length later in our conversation.

When asked what was the most significant change that had taken place in his lifetime he thought that possibly it was the present ease of communication, in particular the motor car. He remembered that it was traditional for his mother to shop in Kirkham, always on Friday, this outing proving a major event in the household. For provisions that couldn't be carried in a shopping basket they relied on visiting tradesmen. Three different Co-operative Societies – Blackpool, Kirkham and Longridge – serviced the needs of the village communities, firstly with horse drawn vehicles and later motorised transport. He remembered well the handwritten receipts from each transaction which would be carefully stuck into a book and then presented on 'dividend' day (the accumulated discount given by the Co-operatives to their registered customers over a period of time) in exchange for cash. He also remembered the Hardware van which called weekly, stocked with almost everything needed on the farm, hand tools, nails, scythes, and the inevitable paraffin – required for home heating, hanging lights in the home and shippons, incubating eggs in chicken rearing and so many other uses.

This he said was the age of re-cycling. Up to the 1950s no local authority ever collected a dustbin in the village. Household food scraps were used to feed the pig, compostable materials were composted, papers were carefully straightened and bundled, kept to provide squares for the outdoor privvy and combustible material for the daily chores of lighting house fires and boilers, both for hot water for washing and for cooking pig swill. He reiterated that almost everyone would keep a pig which would be killed by Harry Ward of Rhododendron Cottage (famous for his topiary garden which regularly attracted 'Mystery (or 'misery') Tour' coaches from Blackpool in the late '50s and '60s) and who was Chief Slaughterman at Preston Abattoir. Marshall well remembered helping his mother make 'black puddings' following such an event.

Like many in the Parish he had his own memories of the days when Isaac Ball's Burrell Steam Engine would arrive with its threshing set, but Marshall said that these engines were so heavy that they quickly accounted for the concrete in the farm yards, concrete which had been laid thinly to cover the cobbles which had been the basis of almost every yard in the Parish. He also recalled the carnage which followed the demolition of the stacks in the stack yard. These were the home to countless rats and mice which were quickly despatched by a plethora of men, children, dogs of all breeds and descriptions and the farm cats. He didn't think that Health & Safety would approve of the wild goings on at these events, with the added danger of wildly brandished hayforks by men and children alike!

Another area of his early life was revealed when he described the annual influx of migrant workers, usually from Ireland, who would come from their own crofts to help with the various seasonal crops which needed to be gathered. The same men returned year after year to the same family farms and were accommodated wherever they could find a place to sleep. He reminded me that the Fylde was once one of the country's largest egg producing regions but was also self-sufficient in producing its own animal foodstuffs, grain, root crops (Mangels, turnips, potatoes) for the mixed farms of the time. Harvesting of these crops would be done by the Irishmen, as well as the major annual tasks such as making hay. He remembered one such migrant, a John Cafficky (he thought that was how it was spelt, but wasn't sure) who hailed not from Eire but Northern Ireland and being a staunch Orangeman would not eat at the same table as his Southern brethren. Times, it seems, change little. He was impressed with John Cafficky however, who was a very skilful man capable of fashioning beautifully decorative articles from paper.

There were also what Marshall called the *'Men on bicycles'* who frequented the village. Some of these are described elsewhere in this history, but Ike Fenton stands out in his memory for Ike was a professional rat-catcher, travelling with poisons (no doubt no longer allowed) from farm to farm, pursuing his calling. There were also *'bike-men'* following such diverse trades as mole-catching to knife-sharpening but all making a simple living from the needs of the Parish communities.

One tragic event stands out for him, the destruction of a large old brick barn at Roseacre Hall Farm, sometime in the 1950s. This, farmed by the Pickervance family got on fire, trapping a variety of animals which were confined within its walls. He recalled that the whole community turned out to help and evacuated the cattle easily enough. However, the liberated pigs had other ideas and dashed back to their home, which was now an inferno. Fortunately they were persuaded to come out again and there were no known fatalities.

Taxed regarding outstanding *'characters'* from Roseacre he said that there had indeed been a few. He then told me of Bob Bennett's (Church Commissioners Work Force) cousin, Dicky, who lived in a small cottage in Roseacre with his sister Elizabeth Ann. Dicky it appears was a *'romancer'* and *'exaggerator'* famous for his tall stories. Marshall illustrated this trait by saying that Dicky had once been describing a crop of mangels, saying that *"They were so big they had to be cut into four before anyone could carry them away"*. Dicky it seemed was married, but his wife didn't live with him, choosing instead to reside at Roseacre Farm, where she was housekeeper to Sam Salthouse. This seemed an amicable arrangement but the couple would occasionally be seen going on an evening outing together. Meanwhile Dicky lived with his sister, Lizzie Ann, who was reported to be *'strange'*, a rather gaunt woman, with very few teeth. Dicky served in the British Army throughout the First World War and was a member of the British Expeditionary Force and returned home with a legacy of ill health, probably as a result of being gassed. Dicky, like most of his era wore clogs clad with what Marshall described as *'Cokers'* or clog irons. Despite having irons to protect them the middle of the wooden soles

were prone to wear and Dicky would tack crossbars of material to the soles to prolong their life. He would also repair any holes in the sole by pushing in spent matchsticks or nails.

Sam Salthouse, however, was Marshall's favourite *'character'*. He was the *third* generation *'Sam'* Salthouse, his grandfather known locally as *'Old SAM'*, his father, *'Young SAM'* and Sam himself as *'Old young un'*. He probably deserved this description because, as Marshall said, he always looked old throughout his life. He liked a drink and was often worse for wear because of it. When once asked why he had never married, he replied that he could *"never remember the woman he had been out with the night before!"* Marshall remembered that he was never very competent with motorised vehicles, but he passed his driving test sometime after the Second World War, ensuring that he passed by leaving half a pig carcass on the back seat of his car for the examiner.

His first tractor was a grey Ferguson and it is told in local lore that the first time he drove it he was seen heading towards a pond shouting *"Whoa lass, whoa"*, ending up stalled in the mud on the edge of the pond. Marshall was privy to another of his tractor escapades. He apparently swapped his grey Fergie for a new red Massey-Ferguson and was driving this down a bumpy local lane one day, far too fast and being thrown about so that his feet were neither in contact with brake or clutch. As he passed Marshall he shouted, *"A reckon nowt o' these red buggers!"*

He was driving his car down the street in Roseacre one day on his way home from the Boot & Shoe Public House at Elswick, when the car caught fire. Legend has it that he left the car, rode his bike back to the pub and engaged an Elswick car mechanic, who had been drinking with him, to return to Roseacre to look at the car. Fortunately when they returned, the fire, probably an electrical fault had gone out of its own accord.

Marshall in his researches on Roseacre spoke with one of Sam's neighbours, Ivan Stafford, (now living at Great Eccleston) who recounted a tale put about by Sam following his return from hospital in 1976. The incident occurred during a summer heat wave, when Sam was rushed unconscious to the old Preston Infirmary with pneumonia. It must be recorded that the heat wave was having disastrous results, particularly on many of the elderly and the Accident & Emergency sections of the hospital was unable to segregate all the casualties into male & female wards. Ivan said that Sam had told him that when he at last recovered consciousness he discovered a scantily clad woman in the bed on his right and a similar sight on his left. *"B. . . Hell, I've finally gone to Heaven"* was said to have been Sam's retort.

Ivan also told Marshall an anecdote of his own. He was cutting his hedge one day when Sam passed and stopped for a chat. When Ivan told

Treales Church Group circa 1910.
*Front Row*: G. Barnes, A. Cowburn, H. Ward, J. Richardson, A. Robinson, J. Ball, C. Fisher, J. Cowburn; *Centre*: R. Birkett, E. Birkett, ?, L. Sanderson, M. Sanderson, M. Sudell, M. Butler; *Back Row*: J. Ball, ?, B. Ward, Rev. Allen, A. Marquis, L. Cowburn, S. Cowburn, J. Birkett, J. Ward, N. Cowburn

Sam that he was trying to sort out his hedge before it rained and didn't have time to chat, Sam took umbrage and told Ivan that, *"He'd never do out with his hedge, and it needed rippin out"* and the trouble with *'his sort'* was that they never had time for the old; that it was awfully lonely at his age, no one visiting him any more! As he was saying this in a whining, aggrieved voice, a car drew into Sam's drive and the driver started to blow the horn, *"It looks as though you've got company, Sam"*, said Ivan, *"Well b-gg-r me"*, said Sam, *"I never gets a minutes peace. One lot goes and another lot turns up. I'd best be going or they'll a supped all me ale!"* Then he paused and looked at Ivan long and hard and said, *"Thee b… hedge still wants rippin out"*.

We both had a good laugh at the ways of the elderly and then wondered where the morning had gone.

✧✳✧✳✧✳✧

### CHRIST CHURCH, TREALES

The church has for years been the hub of this widespread parish. Built on land bequeathed by the Derbys it was constructed in 1855 and received its first incumbent in 1858, the Reverend Joseph Hodgkin. It is surrounded with its graveyard which has been extended once in the lifetime of the building.

The church itself is a simple structure, stone built with a steep pitched roof and simple lancet windows, the external walls between the windows with buttresses. It has an added porch and chancel. It boasts a bell tower with one bell. The serene interior with painted barrel roof, has exposed brick on the wall between the nave and chancel.

The vicarage stands in its own grounds to the North of the church, a large brick built house in the style of most of the estate property. However, with the departure of the Reverend Philip Maddock in 1996, this good

Christ Church, Treales, showing the original interior before modification in the 1960s.

Arthur. The late Mrs. Kitty Wright was his housekeeper.
*From 1944 - 1947 Christ Church Treales was in the care of Kirkham Parish*
*1947-1954: Rev'd Speakman*

Married with 2 children, Mr. Speakman came to Treales after the Second World War and moved to Bolsover in 1954.
*1954-1968: Rev'd McKenley Cameron*

Married with one daughter Mr. Cameron opened a Youth Club and tennis courts at Treales and was much respected for the work he did in the Parish.

family home became empty and is now the subject of a planning permission application by the Church Commissioners to convert it into multiple dwellings. These plans have received certain objections mainly on the grounds of dangerous access and sight lines and in co-operation with the Parish Council the developers have agreed to re-think that part of the application to which the objection applied. A list of the incumbents from 1858 has been researched and is printed below:-

*1858-1898: Rev'd Joseph Hodgkin*

Although the first priest at Treales, little is known about Mr. Hodgkin. His signature is on minutes of Education Meetings of the period but no other articles/memorabilia have been found locally or by the Records Office in Preston.

*1899-1902: Rev'd John Barker*

Again records concerning Rev'd Barker are very few. It is known that he was Priested in 1893. He then became Curate at Kirkham and Vicar of Ribby with Wrea in 1902.

*1902-1944: Rev'd H. J. Allen*

Rev'd Allen is remembered by some parishioners as the Vicar who had a pony and trap and rode a bicycle. He was married with one son,

*1968-1969: Canon Cookson*

Canon Cookson came from Barton for one year at Treales.
*1969-1974: Rev'd Clifford Carver*

The Rev'd Carver, a bachelor, had no transport and was often to be seen walking round the Parish. He claimed that actually he never walked very far because 'lifts' were so plentiful.
*1975-1987: Canon Godfrey Ian Hirst*

Full of life and humour Godfrey's ebullient personality permeated the whole parish. During his stay at Treales he became an Honorary Canon of the Cathedral and his energetic approach to his 'other job', Industrial Mission, proved to be very successful. At this time the vestry was refurbished, making very much better storage space for vestments, etc. Godfrey still remains a good friend of Treales Church and is now Vicar of St. Cuthbert's, Lytham, and Rural Dean of Kirkham Deanery.
*1988-1996: Rev'd Philip Arthur Louis Maddock*

A sincere and quiet man, Philip combined his work as Priest in Charge at Treales with work for the deaf in the Diocese. During his incumbency much work was done to refurbish the inside of church, the pews being stripped and the whole Church recarpeted.

## 1998-2000: Rev'd Alastair Whyte

Alastair achieved the difficult task of bringing together two parishes of somewhat dissimilar character. His Wesham Parish having generously accepted his part-time involvement at Treales, his increased workload was dealt with patiently and with much good humour.

During this period the church bell was refurbished and we were able to ring in the new Millennium at noon on the first day of the year 2000.

We are grateful to Alastair and Christ Church, Wesham, for accepting and coping so well with the merging of the two parishes.

## THE ORIGINS OF TREALES SCHOOL

The origins of the elementary school at Treales can be found in a legacy of Dr. William Grimbaldeston M.D., of St. Dunstan's in the West, London. In his will, dated 28th September 1725, he bequeathed in trust:

> *"£300 to be invested in land, the income of which was to be applied towards the binding out of poor children as apprentices in Treales."*

By 1814, the numbers of apprentices had for many years been insufficient to use up the whole income. The trustees, therefore, decided to establish a school at Treales. It was built on a piece of waste ground

Treales School circa 1925. (Names as accurate as memory allows)
*Back Row*: Jack Hesketh, Bob Baldwin, Tommy Kay, Jackie Jackson, Windham Hall, Billy Bennett, Charlie Baldwin; *2nd Row*: Mr. Stephenson, Alice Kay, Alice Baldwin, Ivy Jennison, Muriel Clark, Ethel Richardson, Olive Benson, Jenny Hesketh, Alice Rawlinson, Mrs. Lord.; *3rd Row*: Mary Nottingham, Madge Davies, Peggy Suddell, Maggie Cookson, Jenny Hesketh, Alice Rayton, Madge ?, Nellie Hesketh, Annie Massam.; *4th Row*: Peggy Suddell, Grace Parkinson, Jennette Hall; *5th Row*: Billy Porter, Arthur Richardson, ? Massam, Lizzie Sharrock, Nellie Cookson, Heber Clark, John Hall; *Front Row*: Edward Clark, Teddy Porter, Arthur Parkinson, George Tomlinson, Bobby Hesketh, Dick Suddell, Jackie Baldwin, Bobby Armstrong.

owned by Lord Derby, one shilling a year to be paid to him in acknowledgement. The cost of the school and schoolmaster's house was over £269 and a schoolmaster was to be appointed at a salary of 40 guineas. Books for the scholars would be provided at a cost of £1.10s.0d. per year.

Articles of government for the school were drawn up in October 1851. These stated that the children should be taught in accordance with the doctrines of the Church of England and that the schoolmaster should teach all the children coming from the hamlets of Treales, Roseacre and Wharles. They would be taught reading, writing and accounts. Those children who were able to pay would give the master 4d a week for learning to write and 8d a week for learning accounts. Those unable to pay would be taught gratis. It was stated that the schoolmistress would teach the girls plain sewing and knitting without charging a fee.

As further payment the master and mistress were paid 'cockpennies' and the children also paid fire money for the use of the school only. 'Cockpennies' refers to the practice of one penny being returned to scholars when they paid their fees. This penny was expected to be staked on a school cockfight, which took place annually at Shrovetide. This gradually changed to a fee to be paid at Shrovetide to the master.

The school opened in 1816 with an average of 70 pupils attending, none requiring free instruction.

### The School Buildings

The first school at Treales (School House Farm opposite the present building) was completed in 1816 at a cost of £269.15s.6d. A Mr. William Brown was paid £162 for the work.

This school pre-dates the church at Treales and the school children took part in celebrating the beginning of the building work on the church. At a meeting of the trustees on July 11th, 1853, it was resolved that:

> "The sum of £5 be given towards a treat to the children of
> Treales School on the occasion of laying the foundation
> stone of Christ Church, on the 7th inst."

In 1858 there began a long campaign to build a new schoolhouse, garden and premises on condition that Lord Derby erect a new schoolhouse with master's residence. A long wait ensued until a letter from Mr. Doble, Assistant Inspector of Schools, dated June 16th 1871 threatened to remove the school from the control of the trustees unless assurance of the renewal of the school premises was made.

As a consequence, a tender for £1071 was accepted and the new school opened in 1874 under the guidance of the schoolmaster, Mr. Thomas Chorley. Gates and railings for the new school had already been purchased, as had thirty fruit trees for the orchard.

Apart from the addition of office facilities, kitchen and inside lavatories, the school premises remained much the same until the building of new offices and a classroom for the use of infants in 1994. The school would now have its own hall, created from the former Junior classroom. The former air raid shelter in the playground was demolished at this time.

### Attendance

At the present time (March 2000) there are 53 pupils attending Treales School. The number of scholars has been between 30 and 60 children for most of the last sixty years. During the Second World War the local pupils were joined by children evacuated from Salford. In the first hundred years of Treales School, it seems to have been the case that between seventy and a hundred children were on the register. The plans for the school built in 1872 were such as to provide accommodation for 104 children. These numbers reflect the larger population of Treales at this time (about double the present day) and the fact that most of the children stayed for their entire school career.

The discrepancies between the numbers on roll and the actual figures seem to have been a constant source of anxiety for Mr. Chorley. There are numerous entries in the school logbook detailing reasons for non-attendance and recording visits by the Attendance Officer.

The ravages of diseases such as measles, mumps, scarlet fever, whooping cough, chicken pox and diphtheria are well documented. There is also the occasional poignant entry recording the absence of the headmaster attending the funeral of one of the schoolchildren. A child of the Butler family of Stud Farm, died when Typhoid occurred at the school. The school was closed for a time and the water-tank condemned and replaced.

In a more light-hearted vein (though viewed with great disapproval by the headmaster) are the reasons for absences which reflect the changing seasons in the countryside and the demands of farm life where children were such a valued source of labour. Helping with the harvest, gathering mushrooms, planting potatoes, looking for plovers' eggs, hay making, picking up fruit blown from trees on a windy night and helping with the laundry on a Monday, all receive a mention in the log. The difficulties of walking to school when lanes were water logged or deep in snow account for quite a few absences. One entry, dated February 14th 1876 reads:

> "Very heavy fall of snow in the night. Very few children
> present, the roads being almost impassable. Grouped two
> or three classes together and deviated from the timetable".

The school can never be unaffected by the cycle of the seasons and the farming year, being situated in the midst of the Fylde countryside, and it would not be appropriate to try to separate it from its roots. It is also still affected by the problems created by severe weather conditions as those who remember the snows which necessitated the closure of the school for four days in February, 1996, will testify!

## Curriculum

The original curriculum consisted of *'reading, writing and accounts'* with *'plain sewing and knitting'* being taught to the girls. This, with the religious teaching of Old and New Testaments, the Catechism and the Church's seasons and feasts, constituted the curriculum for most of the 19th century, with later additions being the teaching of aspects of history, geography, drawing and music. When the Trustees met in school they are recorded as having studied the register and heard the children sing.

The present National Curriculum, first introduced in 1988, bears quite close resemblance to this in subjects covered. There has, however, been a much greater emphasis given to science and technology over recent years. One can only speculate as to the reaction of past pupils (and teachers!) to the school's being connected via an Internet to the World Wide Web of cyberspace. Yet one is also struck by the continuity of school life down the years when one sees photographs of the *'Gardening Club'* from 70 years ago, looking remarkably similar to the ones taken recently of Treales school children working hard to improve their pond and wildlife area.

It is comforting to realise that Treales C. of E. School, although part of the growing trend towards globalisation of knowledge, still retains its roots and derives its values from the church and community which it serves. Long may it continue to enjoy the best of both worlds.

### Members of Staff 2000

#### Teaching Staff
Mrs. Sandra Wright ............... *Head Teacher and Infant Teacher*
Mr. Christopher Shields ........ *Junior Teacher*
Mrs. Anne Watson ................. *Part-time Teacher*
Mrs. Sandie Wright .............. *Specialist Teacher Assistant*
Mrs. Deborah Fellows ........... *Nursery Nurse (Special Needs)*
Mrs. Elizabeth Jenkinson ....... *Non-teaching Assistant*
Mrs. Marie Taylor ................... *Non-teaching Assistant*
Mrs. Elizabeth Haines ........... *Nursery Nurse (Special Needs)*
Mrs. Sally Howes ................... *Nursery Nurse (Special Needs)*

#### Administrative Staff
Mrs. Sandie Wright ............... *Secretary*

#### Lunchtime Staff
Mrs Jean Bass ........................ *Dinner Supervisor*

Mrs Sylvia Braithwaite ........... *Dining Room Assistant*
*Welfare Assistant*
Miss Maria Bass ..................... *Welfare Assistant (Special Needs)*
Mrs. Elizabeth Jenkinson ....... *Welfare Assistant*
Mrs. Susan Fearon ................. *Welfare Assistant (Special Needs)*

#### Maintenance
Mr. Peter Tranter ................... *Site Supervisor*

### THE PARISH FIELD DAY
#### Introduction

In this Millennium year the parish has decided, as part of its celebrations, to reinstate its traditional Field Day. Promoted by the Millennium Committee this was held on 1st July, and it is hoped that this event should once again become an integral part of the parish calendar of entertainment.

To put the Field Day into perspective we asked Dorothy Hall, one time secretary and treasurer to the Field Day Committee, if she was able to tell us more about this important day in the life of the community? Not only was she able to tell us about the Field Day during the period when she served on the committee but she was able to produce archive material, from which this article has evolved, dating back almost a century.

#### Earlier times

The earliest record we have of the event is the Field Day Account Book beginning, in the year 1913. This gives a continuous record of the Field Day committees accounts up to the onset of the Second World War in 1939 when the event was in abeyance. Accounts recommence in 1946 and continue until 1956. The book does show accounts for the war years but is only concerned with the renting of the field (on which the Field Day was held) to J. J. Richardson and several minor sums paid to T. Bennett for cutting thistles, mending gate and fencing, for which he received fourteen shillings and ten shillings respectively. It would also seem that the field was kept free of moles at the *'Mole Rate of 6d'*. However, perhaps the most fascinating insight into the organisation and format of the Field Day is to be found in another of Dorothy Hall's treasures, the Field Day Minute Book commencing April 12th 1937.

#### Parishioners meetings

As stated above, the earliest record available of a meeting of parishioners to debate the Field Day was dated April 12th 1937. This meeting was held in the school, the chairman being the Vicar, the Reverend H. J. Allen. The following were appointed to serve on the committee; *Rev. H. J. Allen, Messrs. A. Pickervance, J. Benson, A. Hall, H. Hall, T. Iddon, T.*

Ball, J. Hogarth, J. Fisher, H. Ward, J.R. Ball, A. Parkinson, W. Sharrock, P.W. Hall, H. Black, R. Swan, H. Wright and Mrs Ingle (it would seem that this was heavily weighted in favour of male opinion).

It was agreed at this meeting that Coronation Celebrations should be held in conjunction with the Field Day and W. Hale (The Derby Land Agent) who also attended the meeting, reported that the Lancashire County Education Committee proposed to make a grant for mugs to be presented to each child as a memento of the coronation. (Each child in the parish received a mug, designed by one of the children in an open competition, to mark the year 2000). The day chosen for the event in 1937 was June 19th.

Further meetings of the chosen committee followed and give interesting insights into the detailed planning undertaken. On April 12th 1937 it was recorded:-

*1) 'that servants subscribing one shilling or more to a collector be given a ticket of admission to the field and tea'.*

*2) 'to engage Kirkham Brass Band and to arrange for the attendance of Dewhurst's Fair'.*

*3) for the date of the Field Day to be advertised in the Lancashire Daily Post of April 15th & 16th.*

On May 10th it was reported that:-

*1) arrangements had been made for the attendance of Connelley's Fair since it was not possible to engage Dewhursts.*

*2) resolved that Mr. Mellor of Kirkham be offered the rights for sale of ice cream at £1.*

*3) That Mr. Cunliffe of Preston be asked to hold the stand for sweets and minerals for a fee of 5/-.*

*4) The cycle stand be let to Mr. J. Parkinson at the same terms as last year. (presumably most came by bicycle and had to leave them somewhere).*

On a more practical note it was resolved to hire help to man the boilers, and to do the washing-up, and several appointments were made: for gatekeepers, stylekeepers, doorkeepers, a clerk to the course, marshall of runners, starter, handicappers for the adult course. The children's handicapper was to be Mrs. Ingle.

At the meeting on June 7th 1937 other practical decisions were made concerning the supply of food and drink for the event, but later in the meeting the discussion turned to who was going to prepare the field and who was to be allowed to compete on the day. On the latter point it was resolved.

*1) 'that it be made clear that competitors for these events must reside or work in the parish (but)*

*2) that any non-parishioners who subscribed 10/- or more should be treated as resident in the parish.*

That the event was meticulously planned is very evident from the further records available via these interesting minutes, and Mrs Hall was able to produce other evidence of the care taken by the then organisers, to ensure that all eventualities were covered, including various insurance documents to safeguard the committee from third party claims.

### The events on Field Day

What surprises most is the athleticism displayed on Field Day,

Field Day procession near Bolton Houses, Treales. Maypole dance team led by their trainer, Mrs. Flitcroft. Alice Marquis and Alice Hall the two leading dancers.

the event being almost a mini Olympic Games. The prizes for the adult section were comparatively generous, usually a first prize of 12/6, second 6/- and third prize 2/6, (1938). Included in the records for that year was a hand-written receipt dated September 6th.

*Field Day 1938, Sept 6th*
*5 hrs. Cutting fenc, setting stoop*
*Received 5/-   Signed T. Bennett*

It would seem that to receive 5/- for five hours work and 12/6 for winning the adult 100-yard race bears some comparison with modern day sporting rewards and the minimum hourly wage.

The format of the 48th annual Field Day and Sports, Saturday June 18th 1938, a copy of which was held by Mrs. Hall, showed that the children's sports were held in the afternoon, the adult races commencing at 6.15pm.

The children's races catered for those aged 5 & 6 years, aged 7-8 years, aged 9-10 years, aged 11-12 years and aged 13-14 years. The events included flat races of 60 and 100 yds, potato and egg & spoon races, and a three-legged race for the most senior children. The prizes were much less than those offered to adults, ranging from a top prize of 1/6d to 3d for a sixth place.

The adult sports included 'open' and 'local' races at familiar events; 100 yards, 220 yards and one mile, but more interesting were the half mile and one mile bicycle races. Whether these were conducted on grass or on road isn't given. Novelty races were included for adults, *'egg & spoon race'* and *'cigarette race'*. Just what this latter entailed isn't stated but it seems very unhealthy if not positively dangerous. The six a side ladies 'tug of war' also seems to have been a serious event, although the prize money at two shillings each for the winners was meagre by comparison.

It would seem that the Field Day was not held during the second world war, which is surprising because in those years the communities relied very heavily on homemade entertainment's, holidays being almost impossible to take for reasons of danger and travel difficulties. The minute's book therefore jumps from 1939 to 1946 when a joint *'Field Day and Victory Celebration Committee Meeting'* was held on June 3rd . The influence of the war period is very evident in that special race categories were available for members of the parish who had been involved in the war time institutions, the A.R.P. (Air Raid Precaution), Home Guard, Firewatchers, W.V.S. (Women's Voluntary Service), the Women's Institute, members of the Armed Forces, and those who had served in the army but were now demobilised.

It is also interesting to see the subtle changes which were taking place in the events, 'Obstacle' and 'Pillow Fights' being included in 1946; and to

the organisation in that in 1947 it was agreed that a Brass Band no longer be engaged but a good quality speaker system be available instead.

In 1949 there appears to have been a marked disagreement between the Field Day Committee and the then Vicar, regarding the use of the school as part of the Field Day venue. The result of this altercation was that it was resolved (June 8th 1949):
*'…to hire a marquee if possible, for teas, etc., the chairman and secretary being authorised to spend £20. on this'.*

This must have been a successful venture for in the minutes for May 4th 1950, a marquee fund was proposed, and agreed that the tent should become the property of the Field Day committee. The committee were also quick to see this as a profit making venture and set a rental charge for hire at:
*'…£3.3s.0d (proposed by P.W. Hall, seconded by W. Kay). The borrowers to be responsible for cartage and any damage'.*

The question of provision of *'conveniences'* on the field (presumably the school was still out of bounds) was discussed in 1957 and a decision made to leave these arrangements to Mr. Ralphs (Clerk of Works to the Church Commissioners). How he solved this problem we do not know.

By 1954 a Ladies v Gentlemen football match had been included, together with 'putting the weight'. 'Slashing the ham' was also featured but it is not described in the minutes so it is uncertain what this entailed.

### In decline

By March 20th 1956 the committee decided that the children's sports would be conducted as in previous years, but that instead of holding adult events in the evening a *'knockout football competition'* would be arranged *between the following teams:- Kirkham, Wesham (Morland Rovers), Treales, Weeton, Lund, Lea, Elswick (Bonds Lane), and Willow Rovers (Kirkham).*

In a very short minute dated 25th March 1957, in almost the last entry in the minute book appeared the following:-
*'A meeting was held in Treales School on March 25th 1957, when through the lack of interest it was decided not to hold a Field Day this year'.*

*H. Wright, Chairman.*

Here the meeting ended.

### Reinstated again

Following the demise of the event through lack of interest in 1957, Mrs Hall was able to tell us that the Field Day was revived by the Vicar and parishioners of Christ Church, Treales, circa 1970, when the event was held in conjunction with the annual Rose Queen and her retinue. However, shortly after its restart, and following objections from a section of the parish not associated with Christ Church, the Field Day once again became a secular event, organised as in earlier days by its own Field Day Committee.

Mrs. Hall recounted that the 'modern' Field Day was a much more simple affair than in earlier days. Refreshments, free to the children taking part, were provided voluntarily by parishioners and prepared in the school on the day of the event. Races were held for the children but other attractions had been added at this time, sideshows of all descriptions being very popular. The expense of the day was defrayed by holding a raffle.

It would seem that there was further dissent within the parish and complaints were lodged with the committee that the older children living within the parish were not being catered for by the Field Day. To counter this claim the committee organised a disco evening, the venue being the barn at Shorrocks Farm, by courtesy of the Stuart familie, and refreshments in the form of 'hot dogs'. Crisps and drinks were provided for those participating. However, a general lack of interest in this event caused the cancellation of the Field Day and the disbanding of the Field Day Committee circa 1986.

### Postscript

With the reinstating once again of the Field Day for the year 2000 it was interesting to see how this years event compared with those held in the past.

The documents relating to the Field Day from earlier times deserve closer scrutiny. Perhaps someone in the parish will be interested in researching this archive material in greater depth and publishing their findings for the instruction of the community? The result could be both educational and entertaining.

✧❀✧❀✧❀✧

## THE VILLAGE CHARITIES

### Ellen Boulton Charity

Of the three charities associated with the parish, (Grimbaldeston & Bridgett being the other two) the Ellen Boulton Charity was specific in its support for the poor of Treales. In existence since 1657 many of its records are held by the County Archivist in Preston. Further foundations were added by other benefactors, John Boulton (1658), Robert Whalley (1664) and later by a John Porter.

Trustees were appointed for the charity in 1857 and its affairs were further regulated by order of the Charity Commissioners in 1889. Its first appointed trustees were Thomas Shaw, Surgeon of Kirkham, together with the Vicar and Churchwardens of Christ Church, Treales. The trustees were charged to distribute the yearly income, less expenses for their management of the charity in one or more specific ways:
*To the relief of the poor of the hamlet of Treales in*
*(i) subscriptions or donations in aid of any*

*(a) Dispensary Infirmary, Hospital or Convalescent Home, upon such terms as to secure the benefit of the institution for the objects of the charity.*
*(b) Provident Club in or near Treales for the supply of coal, clothing or other necessaries.*
*(ii) Contributions for the provision of nurses for the sick and infirm.*
*(iii) The supply of*
*(a) clothes, linen and bedding, fuels, tools, medical or other, and in sickness food or other articles in kind, to an amount not exceeding seven pounds in any one year*
*(b) temporary relief in money by way of loans or otherwise in cases of unexpected loss or sudden destitution.*

The endownment of the charity consisted of 'a tenement called Rabys at Woodplumton'.

It is known that this property was let at the end of the nineteenth century to Mr. John Catterall at £13. per annum. Net income was divided on St. Thomas's day among approximately twenty one persons. None of the claimants were in receipt of poor law relief and only one was really poor. The poor recipient received £5. Others received sums ranging from one shilling to seven shillings. A balance of £4 was held in hand by the trustees for repairs to the property.

In the 1940s, the trustees then in charge of the charity decided that the upkeep and repairs necessary to keep Rabys in good condition were so great that it militated against the spirit of the charity and they decided to sell. Unfortunately the property market at that time was at a low ebb and the sum received was relatively small in investment terms, the charity continues and in recent times has distributed logs or chickens to the elderly or infirm as well as providing a free bus specifically for Christmas shopping. Although the Ellen Boulton Charity only has a small foundation and receives fluctuating returns on its investment the current trustees are determined to continue this ancient and respected part of the heritage of our parish.

### Bridgett Charity

All that is known of this charity is that the amount of £15 was deposited in the New Bank, Preston in 1822, ostensibly by 'Bridgett' but no documentation is in existence to substantiate this. Interest on the £15 was to be paid by the Bank at $4^1/_2$ per cent per annum.

Where the Ellen Boulton Charity was specifically for the poor of Treales, this Bridgett Charity was to be distributed for the benefit of poor persons in the hamlet of *Wharles only*. Those not receiving regular poor relief received sums of one shilling. Occasionally two shillings would be given to a particularly deserving case. Recipients were nominated by the Vicar of Christ Church, Treales. In 1860 the total income from the charity was estimated at 10/- per annum. Nothing more is known of this charity.

## PARISH ACTIVITIES

### Treales, Roseacre & Wharles Branch of the Women's Institute

The Treales Branch of the W.I. was formed seventy eight years ago. The first President to be elected was Mrs. Allen, wife of Rev. Allen, then incumbent of Treales Church. The Vice-President was Mrs. Annie Pickervance and a list of names and addresses of all the founder members is held in the institute records. Obviously the W.I. has changed in its seventy eight years, but Christine Howarth, the branch Vice-President suggests that there are still similarities between those early days and today's meetings: - but also some differences.

*"The format of our association has changed little since it was first formed. It still relies on its educational and social content to inform and amuse its members - speakers on topical subjects, educational outings, group meetings and birthday and Christmas parties, forming the bulk of its activities. Traditionally each W.I. meeting has commenced with those present singing 'Jerusalem' and this is still the case. There is one big difference however, and that is that very few of its current members wear hats, once almost obligatory.*

*Obviously it is now much easier to get to meetings. In earlier years most members would walk or cycle, and attendance was often affected by the weather or seasonal activities such as hay-time or harvest. The motor car has made it much more convenient for members to attend.*

*The local branches of the W.I. still send delegates to County and National Federation meetings and modern communication has eased the difficulties for those attending. In earlier days it was quite an effort to make the long and tedious journey to London for a national meeting.*

*Change and fashion has done most to alter our competitions. Delving into our earlier records it was interesting to see the type of competition that occupied us during those early days:- sock darning, home made handkerchief and cushion cover competitions, knitted gloves or even making a rhubarb pie. We even had glamorous ankle competitions and one to make a working man's supper for sixpence ($2\frac{1}{2}$p in modern currency)! The chosen topics of our guest speakers has also changed. I remember listening to a talk on 'How to be a modern mother' and another on the 'Deportment and Duties of a Smart Hostess'. Nowadays we are more likely to have a speaker who has been to the moon, or at least climbed Everest.*

*The Second World War was the only period in our history when meetings were disrupted and even then we worked tirelessly raising money for the war effort by organising whist drives and bring and buy sales and supporting local boys who had gone to serve their country. We also had special egg collections for Preston Royal Infirmary when eggs where rationed and in short supply.*

*Of course, one or two of our members have spanned most of our long history. Our longest serving President was Mrs. Alice Ward and our oldest serving member up to her death in late 1999 was Dorothy Garlick. She was always a loyal and lively member and continued to attend our meetings almost up to her 100th birthday. Our President and secretary visited her on her 103rd birthday, which she celebrated with some style.*

*The local group has always prided itself on its cohesive nature, all our members contributing in some way to make this a thriving association. We have always sent a delegate to the Lancashire Federation meetings and one of our members was on the winning Lancashire W.I. team in the BBC Town & Country Quiz. Our annual trips have always been popular; at one time this was probably the longest trip taken out of the Parish by any of our members, and on one occasion it is recorded that we had to push the coach to help it get going. We give a warm welcome to anyone wishing to join and hope that we will always uphold the high standards forged in our long history".*

### Treales Athletic Football Club

In 1922, Catforth and District Summer Football League was formed to give local rural communities the opportunity to enter teams to compete and enjoy a game of football on Summer evenings, as due to the nature of their work the young men of the farming communities were unable to play in the afternoons. It was at this time Treales A.F.C. was founded.

Treales continued to play league, cup and friendly games each season, winning the Baron Challenge Cup in 1929 and achieving the double, Baron Cup and League Champions in 1930, when four members of the Baldwin family, local farmers, played on both occasions. Due to lack of support, unfortunately the League was disbanded in 1934.

During this 14-year period the mainstay of Treales Football Club was Harry Wright who worked tirelessly to make the club a success. Such was his enthusiasm he managed to carry on fielding a side arranging friendly matches wherever he could for a further two seasons.

It was Harry who was instrumental in reviving the Summer League in 1947 and Treales was back as strong as ever, Harry continued with his good work up to his death in 1985.

During the early years Treales Football Club was more than just a football team, providing many social events for the village with their money raising activities, Fur and Feather, whist drives, dances, hot pot suppers and whist and dominoes were organised on a regular basis in order to raise the funds required, for example, any injury requiring medical treatment was accompanied by a doctor's bill and loss of work through injury meant loss of wages, which had to be reimbursed. Transport was

Treales Football Team, 1929.

nucleus of players had been loyal to the club, turning up regularly each week, that for their sakes the club would continue for another season and a request was made to the League to extend or abolish the boundaries. This was to be discussed at the next League AGM and if the outcome was negative Treales would have to withdraw from the League.

Struggling through 1962 even with extended boundaries the club managed to field a full team for each match and by 1963 the club was back to full strength.

In the 1940s and 1950s Treales had an ardent following of supporters which helped to also required to convey the team to away matches along with the general running costs of the club, in the 1950s whist drives were held on a monthly basis in Treales School.

In 1958 it was decided to invite people to become Honorary Vice Presidents for a fee of 10/6d, for this they received a Vice President's card and free entry to all home matches for the current season. The fee was dropped to 5/- in 1959.

Treales was again sucessful in winning the Baron Challenge Cup in 1957 and 1958 the only player still living locally who played in both these matches being George Carter. Runners up on several occasions, the only local surviving players of the Treales side in the 1947 Cup Final are John Sanderson and Les Rawstrone.

According to the rules of the League, tight boundaries were imposed on all clubs and only players residing within these boundaries could play for each respective club. In 1961, Treales Football Club was short of local players, finding it difficult to field a full team on occasions. Some players gave short notice when unable to play, or failing to turn up at all and the club was almost disbanded. However, it was finally decided because a small supplement the cost by filling the teams coach when travelling to away matches. From the early 1970s Tom Ibison became involved in the club and again as Harry worked tirelessly to ensure the clubs continued success, he continued with his enthusiasm, even when in later years he suffered failing eyesight until ill health took its toll prior to his death in 1998. Since then, David Pickervance, together with his son Daniel have stepped into the breach and continue to work with the same determination. The Derby Championship 1970, 1982 and 1991, The Billington Challenge Cup 1982 and 1994, Kerrigan Challenge Cup 1996, 1997, Shorrock Challenge Shield 1966, 1969, 1973 and 1974 are some of Treales achievement. There are now four Leagues run by Catforth and District Summer League. Treales Football Club now field two teams.

For almost eighty years Treales Football Club has given pleasure to hundreds of keen footballers who have had the opportunity to enjoy the game. The keenness and team spirit of the players, the right men at the helm, together with the support of the committee members over the years ensures the continued success of the Club, who can boast they are the only surviving Club with the League from that initial launch in 1922.

## GARDENING IN THE VILLAGE
### The Treales, Wharles & Roseacre Parish Council Annual Gardening Competition

This competition was initially suggested by The Parish Council in 1989 and implemented for the first time during the summer of that year. The council appointed as judges well known authorities within the horticultural field, usually Superintendents of Parks & Gardens for Local Authorities. By choosing such experienced arbiters they ensured that all types of garden within the parish would come under fair scrutiny; the judges themselves having overseen the planting of the varying styles of garden layout, e.g. all herbaceous, tree and shrub gardens, rock and scree gardens and the annual bedding garden. The dates of scrutiny were set late in high summer to allow bedding plants to be at their best. The only criteria for the prizes was that the judges would select winners from what could be seen over the hedge, although an experiment allowing judges to enter gardens was tried (and scrapped) for one year. The standard of excellence has been such that judges have often found it difficult to choose between contenders and to overcome some of these difficulties three different categories, i.e. large, small gardens and terraced house gardens, were devised and these are now in place.

In each of the three classes there are awarded First place, Second place and Highly Commended, but only one entry is given the award 'Overall Winner' for which they receive the Mrs. H. Clark Cup. The Parish Council provide cups for the large and small garden categories. The Councillor Alan Cup goes to the winner of the terraced house garden.

Written records of the competition exist from 1989 and winners include, Frank Walker, Mr & Mrs G. Carter, Mr & Mrs H. Hall, Mr & Mrs A. Hall, Mr & Mrs Coxon, Mr & Mrs Park, Mr & Mrs Gardner, Mr & Mrs Cook, Mr & Mrs Knight, Mr & Mrs Morgan, Mr & Mrs J. Rhodes, E & J Slack, Mrs P. Gunn, Mr & Mrs Molloy, Linda Kidd, Mr & Mrs J.A. Hall.

Judges have included Mr Scrivens, Mr Ashton, County Councillor Whittle, Mr T. Williams, Mr. F. Moor, Mr Holmes and Borough Councillor M. Tomlinson.

The Clerk to the Parish Council, Mr Scholes, who keeps the archive records of the competition, makes the interesting comment that when the competition started, small cash prizes were awarded. However, none of the cheques was passed for payment but kept as Trophies by the recipients. It was because of this that certificates replaced cash prizes.

### A village garden open under the National Gardens Scheme:

In 1992, Mike and Pauline Coxon purchased additional land adjoining their home in Treales and sought 'change of use' planning permission to convert the pasture land to garden. Permission was granted by Fylde Borough Council with the support of our parish council, in the same year. They describe below the transition from meadow to the point where they opened their garden to the public for charitable purposes under the National Gardens Scheme on 18th June 1998:

*"Easter 1993 saw the beginning of our scheme and with the assistance of Frank and Alan Walker, a post and wire fence was erected and the front and side boundary hedges and a willow tree removed, which gave Frank ample opportunity to indulge his passion for bonfires. The land was ploughed, levelled, grass seed sown, a low stone wall built to link with the 'old' garden and a greenhouse erected. It was exposed to the full power of the wind and the elements. After every single pane of glass was broken by gales this was moved to a far more suitable position! The framework was now in place to develop a garden.*

*Gradually, as time, weather and money permitted beech boundary hedging was planted, sixty feet of which was immediately eaten by cows and made necessary the erection of a second post and wire boundary three feet further out from the first so that the cows could only eat grass and we could retain our plants. A pond was dug, rustic fencing erected to create separate areas, borders were designed and the garden started to take shape. Complimentary remarks were received from friends, neighbours, and even total strangers who were passing by. Advice, encouragement and numerous plants were received from friends in the village, not to mention several barrow loads of well rotted manure. We were extremely honoured to receive first prize in the Parish Council Garden Competition, which at that time we didn't know existed.*

*We had been aware of the National Gardens Scheme for a few years and had started visiting gardens open under the scheme. It is difficult to think of a more pleasant way of spending an hour or so than wandering around a lovely garden, admiring plants, getting ideas, talking to other gardeners, sometimes being able to buy plants and refreshments - all this and supporting good causes as well. Several friends suggested we should open our garden. Although the garden was taking shape by now we didn't know if it would be accepted for inclusion in the Yellow Book and were rather apprehensive about making enquiries, knowing we would feel embarrassed if we were rejected. However, we decided we would try, and contacted the county organisers for the scheme who advised us that the general criteria for inclusion were that "there should be sufficient to interest the public for about half an hour for people travelling from up to 40 miles away". Ray and Brenda Doldron, the scheme's officers, visited us, were most encouraging, and accepted us immediately.*

*We opened the garden for the first time on Sunday, 28th June 1998, from 1.00 pm to 5.00 pm. The day was one of the very few dry, warm and sunny days we had that year and we were delighted that 178 people visited us. We raised £405.00. One hundred pounds went to Derian House, nominated by Mr. Oliver Melling, who allowed visitors to park in his field opposite, the balance going to the National Garden Scheme which supports Cancer Relief, Hospices, Macmillan Nurses, the National Trust, the Gardeners Benevolent Fund and other worthwhile causes.*

*We enjoyed our day so much and received so many complimentary remarks from our visitors that we have agreed to open on one day each year on a regular basis."*

### A National Collection of Trees:

The National Council for the Conservation of Plants and Gardens (NCCPG) administers the 'National Collection'" scheme in Great Britain. The NCCPG, Patron: The Prince of Wales, who holds one of the 600+ collections at Highgrove, has its Headquarters at Wisley Gardens, Woking, Surrey. Organised through 41 county groups it has one primary objective. *'To safeguard and conserve the rich diverse gene pool of garden plants held within the British Isles'.* The collections are maintained by a broad spectrum of gardening enthusiasts ranging from Botanic Gardens, Horticultural Colleges, Local Education Authorities, Nursery Gardens and private individuals. Each well-researched collection helps to conserve the genetic stability of plants and protects them against gardening 'fashions', disease and extinction, thus ensuring the availability of an abundant variety of plant material for today and for future generations.

On December 6th 1999, Shirley & Joe Lee of Treales Windmill were awarded the status *'National Collection Holders for the Genus Sorbus'* (Mountain Ash trees), having over eighty different species and cultivars in their garden. There are now five National Collections of Sorbus in the British Isles: The Jodrell Bank Arboretum, Cheshire; Viscount Ridley of Boston House, Blagdon, near Newcastle; East Durham Community College, Durham; The National Trust, Winkworth Arboretum, Godalming, Surrey; and Mr & Mrs Lee, Treales Windmill, Treales.

The award of National Collection Holder is given after considerable scrutiny of the plants and garden by the NCCPG Plant Conservation Officers and holders must adhere to strict rules regarding the scientific use of the collections, offer continual research, propagation of materials for plants in danger of extinction and write annual reports on the state of their collection.

## THE VILLAGE FARMING COMMUNITY
### Bolton House Farm, Church Road, Treales

Bolton House was farmed by Arthur and Sarah Hall between 1936 and 1945 approximately. They had 2 children, Windham and Jennet,. Mr. Hall administered the estate for Lord Derby. Milk was bottled at Bolton House. Matthew Parkinson, who farmed at Hale Hall, suggested an exchange of farms with the Halls, and this being agreed, the Parkinsons took up residence at Bolton House.

In 1958 the Parkinsons retired and moved to Esprick, when Bill and Lena Robinson took over the tenancy. The Robinsons came from Claughton, near Garstang, with their children Irene and Brian.

The farm was then approximately 50 acres and the annual rent £7 per acre. They had 35 cows, together with sheep, poultry and pigs. Jimmy Eccleston who lived at Rose Cottage on Church Road, near the School, used to walk his pigs down the road to Bolton House to be served by Robinson's boar.

One of their workers, Dave Smith, was a conscript in the Royal Air Force for his National Service, and now owns Stilefield Farmstore at Freckleton.

In the 1970s Bill and Lena were given the tenancy of Cross Hill Farm, moved up the road, but retained Bolton House as a farm worker's cottage. In 1988 Bill semi-retired and they returned to live at Bolton House.

Fern Cottage which stood next to the farm was demolished in the 1960s.

### Church View Farm, Treales

Church View Farm is the newest farm to be created in the parish. Bill and Kath Salisbury bought 103 acres, acquired from Whitehall Farm when it was broken up and sold in 1990.

Although Kath came from a farming background, Bill had been in the electrical business since 1964. Their house was built in 1993 and the farm has increased in size to 200 acres. It is predominantly an arable farm, but in recent years Bill has started keeping beef animals. Bill and Kath have 4 children, 3 daughters and 1 son. William now helps his father run the farm.

### Cross Hill Farm, Church Road, Treales

In the 1920s Richard Sudell and family lived at Cross Hill Farm. His son Harry, lived at Rose Cottage with his wife and 4 children. All was not well with Harry's marriage, his wife wanted them to leave the farm and move to St. Annes. Farming at the time was not good and this had been exacerbated by weeks of inclement weather. This proved too much for Harry and sadly in 1931 he took his own life, drowning himself in a pit. Heber Clark from Stud Farm found his body. In consequence, the Sudell

Sheep shearing at Cross Hill Farm circa 1985.

family left Cross Hill Farm and their tenancy was taken by the Richardson family until 1970.

In 1970 Bill and Lena Robinson were appointed tenants in a move with their children, Brian and Irene from Bolton House. The land of the two farms was amalgamated, to make a total of 160 acres. They kept cows, sheep, beef and pigs. Over the years more land was acquired from neighbouring farms; Manor House, Ash Tree, Cross Lane, School House and Stud Farm, increasing the acreage to 300.

In 1978 a new dairy unit was built. Bill and Lena Robinson took semi-retirement in 1988 and moved back to Bolton House. Brian and his wife Jennifer took over the tenancy and moved to Cross Hill with their 3 sons, Mark, Matthew and Andrew. In 1990 Cross Hill was purchased outright by Brian and Jennifer.

### Derby Lodge Farm, Roseacre

The first tenant of Derby Lodge Farm was John Hesketh in about1866.

In 1937 Janey Towers took over the tenancy from the Rawlinsons. Janey's husband had unfortunately died and she had been forced to leave Church Field Farm at Tunstall. One of the conditions of her taking the tenancy of this 175 acre property was that mains electricity was supplied to the farm.

A mixed farm, the stock included 50 cows and poultry. Derby Lodge was the first farm in Lancashire to have a 'Grey Fergie' tractor and Harry Ferguson went to the farm to demonstrate it personally. Isaac Ball used to do the threshing as he did on many of the farms in the area.

In 1945 George Marshall Towers married Mary Walton of Staining, and they moved to the farm in 1946. During the war a plane missed HMS Inskip and landed in a field at Derby Lodge and it was kept under police guard for the night.

George and Mary's son, Marshall, and his wife later took over the farm and in the early 1990s they bought it, subsequently selling it to Jim and Grace Thornley, who are currently farming it with their two children Rachel and Andrew.

One remembered character who frequented the area was 'Tar Jack'. He used to go round tarring cabins in exchange for bed and board. He always managed to stay immaculately clean of tar.

### Grange Farm, Treales Road, Treales

John Melling and his wife Hannah came from Catterall near Garstang in 1893, to farm at Grange Farm, Treales. They had two children, Sarah aged 9, and James aged 7. A second daughter, Jennet was born two years later.

Horses were almost more numerous than cattle in those days, both light and heavy horses being bred every year.

James attended Treales School and later went to Kirkham Grammar School, then near to the Parish Church. He went to school on his donkey.

Sarah married Arthur Hall of Bolton House Farm, Treales, and they had two children, Windham and Jennet. Jennet did not marry and lived at Grange Farm all her life, where she kept poultry and Angora rabbits.

John Melling died in 1919 and James took over the tenancy. In 1920 he married Alice Tomlinson of Clifton Village and in 1922 John Melling was born at Grange Farm. Horses were phased out and replaced by more cows and sheep. Cheese was made for a few years. John Melling walked across the field to Clifton School, it being slightly nearer than Treales. He later cycled daily to Kirkham Grammar School along with Bob Hesketh, Victor Ball, James Richardson (Cross Hill) and three Gardner boys from Catforth. In 1948 John married Gwen Towers of Borwick, near Carnforth, and when James and Alice retired to Fulwood John and Gwen took on the tenancy of Grange Farm.

The milking herd was now about seventy, and lack of buildings restricted any further expansion. Two children were born to the couple,

Alison in 1950 and Oliver in 1953, and 1953 also saw the death of James.

Lord Derby sold the Fylde Estate to the Church Commissioners in 1955, which precipitated a rent increase, but under the Commissioners it was possible to have repairs to property and new buildings at the request of the tenants. Their agent visited all the farms and improved many of the farmhouses, which were in need of renovation. The Commissioners also had the policy of amalgamation which meant that if a farmer retired or died and there was no son to succeed, the farm was not re-let to another tenant, but was added to the farm adjoining. This worked very well for some, but for many young farmers in the parish keen to make a start on the farming ladder, this policy was unfortunate.

In 1966, Grange Farm's acreage increased to 260 acres. A further change in the Estate ownership occurred in 1972, the Church selling to

Grange Farm, Treales. Isaac Balls' threshing set circa 1900.

the Pension Fund Property Unit Trust and the farms acreage increased further to 373 acres, with an almost inevitable increase in the milking herd to 150 the following year. Steady improvements were made to the farm, (new silos and cubicles) until John and Gwen retired in 1980, handing over the tenancy to Oliver, the fourth generation of the Melling family to farm there. Oliver was to marry Helen Mallinson of Bagshot in Surrey in 1982. They have three children, John James and Genevieve. In 1992 Oliver and Helen Melling purchased their farm on the dispersal of the estate by Mountleigh.

John Melling died on June 3rd 2000, aged 77 years.

### Hale Hall Farm, Salwick Road, Wharles

Hale Hall Farm was farmed by Matt Parkinson in the 1930s, but in 1945 he decided he wanted to take things easier and asked Windham Hall of Bolton House Farm to swap. This they did and Windham, his wife Anne, nee Richardson, formerly of Cross Hill Farm, and their three children, Alan, David and Sarah, moved to Hale Hall Farm.

Manor House Farm, Bolton Houses, Treales.

Their sons, Alan and David took over the business and the farm grew, land being incorporated from Shorrocks Farm, Stanley Lodge and Stud Farm and other surrounding farms. Alan and his wife Eileen currently live at Hale Hall; they have two sons, Andrew and Simon, who both work on the farm. David and his wife Dorothy who have two children, Susan and David, live at Stanley Lodge.

### Manor House Farm, Church Road, Treales

Tom and Esther Sanderson moved to Manor House from Ash Tree Farm, Moorside, Treales. Their niece Alice, lived with her parents, Mr and Mrs Tom Marquis, in a cottage in Mowbreck Lane, Wesham. When her mother died Alice was six years old, and she then went to live with Uncle Tom and Auntie Esther at Manor House Farm. When she grew up she met Billy Baldwin, who worked at Mowbreck Hall Farm. The Baldwins had originally come from Tarleton. Alice and Billy were married in 1937 and went to live at Manor House with Tom and Esther. In 1939 Tom died, but Esther continued to live with Alice and Billy, until she died in 1960.

The farm was approximately 70 acres and they had cows, pigs and hens. In 1938 Alice gave birth to twins, Alan and Essie, Billy retired in 1970 and bought the house and buildings and 1.6 acres from the Church

Commissioners, the barn and orchard across the road were offered but turned down. This large brick barn was subsequently demolished. Their other land was divided between Robinsons at Cross Hill and Sandersons at Mee Farm.

Billy died in 1984 and Alice in 1987. Their daughter Essie, moved into the farmhouse in 1985 and still lives there with her husband Alan Lennard. In 1998 they sold the barn at the back of their house to David Webster and Karen Baugh, who are converting it into a house.

### Mee Farm, Moorside, Treales

In 1921 John and Betsy Jane Sanderson took over the tenancy of Mee Farm from the Hargreaves family. Before her marriage, Betsy Jane, was a Richardson, who lived at Rose Hill Farm, Wharles. John and Betsy Jane had 5 children, 4 boys and 1 girl, who all attended Treales School. They told how, at dinnertime, Johnny their son would go poaching and was often late back for his lessons. He and his friends were only ever caught once and Johnny managed to talk his way out of it.

The Sandersons have always milked at Mee Farm, originally with Shorthorns and later Friesians. Before mains water came to the farm, as late as 1945, there was a well. However, the water supply to the well and other pumps in the area was contaminated and for a time the milkman would deliver water to the farm in milk kits. A wind pump was then installed and this was shared with Heights Farm next door. As on other farms, horses were used for the field work and Johnny remembered working with them when only 8 to 10 years old.

During the war, German Prisoners of War worked on the farm. They also had three evacuees (children moved from their own homes because of the danger of wartime bombing and rocket raids) and in recognition of this John and Betsy Jane received a letter from the Queen, thanking them.

During 1927/28 they produced cheese on the farm and the milk would be taken to Pyes Dairy in Kirkham. In the 1940s they remembered two severe winters with snow up to 7 feet deep down Moorside. It was a struggle to get the milk away from the farm and so, once again, they made cheese.

Cows were taken to Preston Auction in a converted lorry, which was pulled by a horse. They told an interesting story of how during the War, Terry Thomas, the actor, would visit the farm and once wanted his photograph taken milking a cow. Other times he would send his chauffeur in a Rolls Royce to pick up supplies. The Sandersons would butcher their own pigs and lambs and people would come from all over to pick up supplies. One man even came in a hearse from Blackpool.

All four of John and Betsy Jane's sons became farmers. Johnny married Grace in 1948 and their sons Ronnie and Alan were born in 1950 and 1956. They lived in Clifton until they moved to Mee Farm in 1966. Ronnie moved to a farm at Longton, Preston, in the 1980s with his wife and family, and Alan and his wife Sue, moved to Mee Farm in 1990, when John and Grace retired. They have 2 children Rachael and Caroline.

### The Evacuees of Mee Farm

In the autumn of 1999, two ladies arrived at Mee Farm and introduced themselves as Margaret and Marion. They had been evacuated during the Second World War along with their sister Irene and brother, Albert Arnot. They came from Swinton, Manchester. Margaret was only five years old and Marion was six. It was sixty years since they had been evacuated so they had decided to take a trip back down memory lane.

Margaret, Marion and Albert were sent to Mee Farm and Irene was sent to Rhododendron Cottage but cried so much for her brother and sisters that Betsy Jane (known as Janie to her family) agreed to let her stay at Mee Farm as well.

Margaret said that Janie taught her how to bake and to this day she is called upon to bake for local events. She and Marion recalled using a small garden fork to weed between the stone sets from one end of the farmyard to the other and said how the weeds at the beginning had started growing again when they reached the end!

Their parents used to come and see them while they were at the farm, getting off the train near what is now the Boy's Brigade and walking to the farm. Their father worked in a factory in Manchester and brought some of the products made there for John, Janie and their family and Janie gave them eggs and meat to take home in return.

When they arrived at the farm, Arthur was only one year old and thought of them as his older brother and sisters. He cried when they went home again after the war.

Margaret and Marion spoke of how kind the family were to them and how much they enjoyed being here in spite of having to leave their parents at such a young age.

The ladies had a look around the farm and I was impressed by how much they remembered in spite of how young they were when they were here. Lots of things have changed and they recalled what used to be where. They had a good chinwag and reminisced about old times, and returned back to the train station with bags full of cooking apples from Mee Farm trees for their beloved baking!

### Moorfield Farm, Treales Road, Treales

The following article appeared in the *'Preston Guardian'* February 23rd, 1895 about Moorfield Farm, which had been built in 1887.

*'Mr. Clayton's farm at Treales, standing back as it does fron the main road, has a commanding appearance. It is on Lord Derby's Estate and has not been built long. Mr Clayton carted all the materials for the buildings himself. The house stands to the front and has a broad carriage drive leading up to it, the farm buildings being at the rear. A large number of young trees have been planted at the front and these in a few years will afford ample protection from the biting winds. I found Mr. Clayton at the rear where the farm buildings are, all of modern design and forming a square. The farmyard was covered with straw so that it would be better for the horses to walk upon. Mr. Clayton goes in for grazing, does not plough or keep any heavy horses. He keeps a capital light legged stock, all thorough breds and has carried off honours on the turf. There have been no foals dropped as yet on the farm.*

*Discussing the current depression Mr. Clayton saw no means whereby it can be relieved especially whilst there is such distress in our large towns. He never knew wheat so low before and instanced a neighbouring farmer selling it at 10 shillings per windle\*. Had not the straw sold fairly well there would not have been the slightest profit on the growing'.*

\*a windle is a plaited basket of dry straw or grass.

After the Claytons left the Garlick family were given the tenancy of

Moorfield Farm in 1900. Will Garlick, his son Dick and his wife Dorothy farmed at Moorfield until 1966, when they retired to Lea Town. They were the first farmers in the area to keep a pedigree Friesian Herd, their prefix being 'Treales'. They held a dispersal sale in 1965, but the prefix is still held by their daughter Freda Richardson who farms at Weerdon House, Catforth. They were one of the first families to import Friesian stock from Canada in 1946. One of the highlights of Will and Dorothy's life at Moorfield was the installation of electricity in 1939.

Will died in 1976, Dick in 1996, and Dorothy late in 1999 at the age of 103. She just missed living through the whole of the twentieth century.

Moorfield is now a private residence lived in initially by the Blackburns and now by the Rickson family.

### Moss House Farm - Moss Lane East Treales

George & Mary Ellen Hogarth moved to Moss House Farm in 1920. They had 5 children who all worked at home on the farm. It was a mixed 130 acre farm and the stock included cows, sheep, pigs and hens. The hen cabins were scattered around the fields and in winter they would go round them all with a Tilley lamp in order to extend the hours of daylight. James, their son, married Elsie in 1930 and took over the running of the farm in 1935. They had 4 children, Raymond,

Moorfield Farm, Treales, showing its broad carriage drive. Now a private residence.

Irene, Christine and Pat. Christine remembered a very happy childhood with their hardworking, loving parents.

In the 1950s they got another 70 acres from Derby Farm. They employed several workers at the farm, including John Gornall from Prospect Cottage, Nen Nicholson from Treales and Harry Fare from Wharles.

James's brother Tom, who was a bachelor, also worked and lived at Moss House Farm. Tom opened a butchers shop on Talbot Road, Blackpool, to sell the meat from the farm. At first they would butcher the animals in the farm kitchen, but Elsie became fed up with the mess and put a stop to it.

The men on the farm undoubtedly worked very hard, and so did the women. Elsie's life revolved around making sure all the meals were on the table on time. With 9 or 10 mouths to feed at every meal it was hard work.

Once a week she would make enough butter to see them through the week. The provin rep. would deliver a bag of flour for her to make all her own bread, and there were always pies and cakes on the table.

Elsie did have a helper, Annie Cookson, in the house. Annie was a hard worker and like a second mother to the children. The Co-op vans used to call with provisions and later Stan Cross used to call with his grocery van. On a Monday they would light the boiler in the wash house; they would start with the whites, then the coloureds, and then the dirty work clothes. They ironed with an electric iron on the kitchen table. They only did the washing once a week.

Raymond was called up for National Service and spent some time in Tripoli. When he was demobbed and returned to the farm, his father flew the Union Jack from the barn. Raymond married May in the 1950s and he took over the farm in 1967. They had 3 daughters. They bought the

T. HOGARTH,
*High-class Family Butcher.*

Always a Prime Selection of
ENGLISH BEEF, MUTTON, LAMB
and PORK.
DRESSED POULTRY from OUR
FARMS **A SPECIALITY.**
Private Address :
**MOSS HOUSE FARM,
TREALES, NR. KIRKHAM.**
ALSO 63, TALBOT ROAD, BLACKPOOL.

*Orders promptly attended to and delivered*
*QUALITY IS OUR MOTTO.*

Hogarths of Moss House Farm, Treales, sold their own produce through a retail outlet at 63, Talbot Road, Blackpool, pictured here.

farm when the estate was broken up and later sold it to John & Jill Gardner and their 3 children, Edward Fiona and Sally.

### New Hall Farm, Wharles

In the 1930s New Hall was farmed by the Nuttall family. They had approximately 10 children. Unfortunately in 1939, Mr. Nuttall died of pneumonia and sadly his widow and children had to leave the farm, moving to Inskip.

In February 1942, Daniel and Hannah Carter took the tenancy of the 250 acre farm. They had previously farmed 101 acres at Upper Rawcliffe. They had 8 children (5 girls and 3 boys) four of whom had left school, but the youngest ones attended Treales School. All their stock was walked from Upper Rawcliffe.

They found no mains water at New Hall. This was a shock as they had been used to mains water at Upper Rawcliffe. At New Hall the water was collected in a large underground tank and then filtered for drinking.

During the war Lord Derby wished *HMS Nightjar* to take New Hall Farmhouse for its use but the Ministry decided to take Shorrocks Farmhouse and land instead.

One farmworker, Tom Alcock, who lived at the *'Eagle and Child'* (which was also a farm), was a member of the Home Guard.

In 1942 there were no tractors on the farm; just 13 horses. Unfortunately all but one of the horses, *'Daphne'*, died of grass sickness, so a Fordson tractor was bought. During the war George and Tommy used to collect pig swill from *HMS Nightjar* after school.

In 1960 George took over at New Hall Farm and he farmed it with his twin brother Tommy, who sadly died in 1982 leaving a widow Pat and three grown up children.

George married Jean Danson (who lived at Lynwood in the Bolton House area of the parish) and they also have 3 grown children.

Over the years New Hall acquired land from several of the

surrounding farms, including Boundary, West View, Shorrocks, Cross Hill and Cross Lane.

In 1991 George and Jean bought New Hall and then subsequently sold it to Mr. Barnes from Bashall Eaves.

Before the Nuttall family lived at New Hall it was farmed by the Massam family who emigrated to Australia. When Mary Massam died her ashes were returned to New Hall to be scattered, as later were her husband's ashes. Before the Massams, a farmer called Robert Ward was tennant.

At Christmas time it was Lord Derby's custom to visit New Hall to buy cheese to take back to Knowsley.

After the war a German named Wilhelm came from Samlesbury to work and live at New Hall.

### Post Farm, Roseacre

Early in the 20th century Post Farm was farmed by the Iddons, followed by the Molloys. When Billy Molloy retired, the tenancy was taken by Peter Fare and his wife Pat in 1971. They had three children, two boys and a girl. Peter had previously farmed at Stanley Grange with his father, but because of the proposed route of the M55 it was feared that Stanley Grange would no longer be a viable farm, and so Peter was given a tenancy at Roseacre.

The farmhouse was built in 1965 after a very old, part-thatched house had been demolished. They recalled that many of the oldest houses and cottages were demolished before preservation orders could be placed on them.

Initially when Peter moved to Post Farm he had an Ayrshire herd, but in the 1980s changed to Friesians. However they still have a few red cows in the herd. All the cows were milked in the shippons until 1994 when a new milking parlour was installed. Like many sitting tenants, the Fare family bought their farm when the Estate was broken up. Their son, Robert, now works at home on the farm.

### Roseacre Hall Farm, Roseacre

In 1919 the tenancy of Roseacre Hall Farm was taken by Thomas and Annie Pickervance from Tarleton. They had seven children, six of whom married local farmers. They walked all their stock from Tarleton, over the River Ribble at Preston to

Roseacre. Their youngest son John took over the tenancy in 1938. In 1919 the farm had 220 acres but in 1941 when *HMS Nightjar* was built the acreage was reduced to 120 acres. However, the land from Stanley Farm, farmed by Bill Shorrock (Harry's uncle) and half the land from Roseacre Farm, rented by Sammy Salthouse, was incorporated into Roseacre Hall Farm in 1968. The farm now has 330 acres.

The farm is a mixed farm. In the early days the milk was taken to Salwick Station by pony and trap. Later it was picked up by the Milk Marketing Board and is now collected by Lancashire Dairies.

John and Agnes Pickervance had four sons, who all farm in the area. Agnes died in 1958 and John married Betty. John retired in 1983 and died in 1990. His youngest son, Harry and his wife Christine took over the

Thomas Carter, Tommy Rigg, Joe Livesey holding David Carter, George Carter, at New Hall Farm, Wharles, c1960.

tenancy. They bought the farm in 1990. They have five children, Thomas, Sonya, Julie, Victoria and Harrison.

When *HMS Nightjar* was built a number of trees were cut down in the middle of a shelter-belt in order that planes could come in to land. This gap is still visible today from Roseacre Hall, a reminder of wartime Britain 1939-1945.

### Rose Hill Farm

Peter Richardson who died in 1879 was known to be a gamekeeper. He lived in Wharles and it must be assumed that he was a gamekeeper to the Derbys before Mr. Kenyon was transferred from Knowsley to Treales to be Head Keeper for the Fylde Estate in 1902. He was the father of Thomas Richardson who with his wife Elizabeth (nee Green) and eight children, farmed at Pointer House, Wharles. The Richardsons took over the tenancy of Rose Hill Farm in 1920 when the then tenants, the Hogarths, moved to Moss House Farm, Treales.

While at Pointer House Farm the Richardsons offered a contracting service to the many small farms in the area, in particular moving manure and hay. This they accomplished with a donkey called 'Ace of Diamonds' and a small cart. When it was suggested that this would have been very hard work for such a light-weight animal it was pointed out that the cart that was used was very small, and the hay fields to be cleared would be no larger than an acre or less.

Rose Hill Farm in 1923 was listed as having approximately 40 acres which supported a small herd of Friesian cows and free range hens which were housed in hen-cabins in the fields.

Tragedy struck the Richardsons in the same year that they moved to Rose Hill when their son, Thomas, died of 'lock jaw' (tetanus) in July of that year. A contemporary newspaper cutting held by the family records that the inquest was held before the deputy coroner Lieut-Col. H. Parker at the 'Eagle and Child'. The inquest was told that the death was due to a simple accident.

*'He told his mother that whilst playing with a potato fork on the Tuesday, his hand slipped and the fork entered his foot'*

The newspaper report told how the boy's condition worsened and he developed convulsions, dying from rigidity caused by tetanus. Verdict: Accidental Death.

Frank died in the 1940s and his wife Elizabeth in 1954 when the tenancy was taken jointly by Arthur and Jim, the partnership known as Richardson Bros., of Rose Hill. The farm grew to 74$^1/_2$ acres with proportionally more cows. The herd was known as a 'Flying Herd'. This was an unusual method of farming at that time; no calves were reared to add to the farm's herd, rather cows were bought in as newly calved and were sold 'in calf'. This ensured that the maximum milk was recovered from each cow in the time that it remained at Rose Hill. The farm also kept 400 free range hens and 6 breeding sows.

Arthur Richardson married Alice Eccleston of Inskip in 1949 and their daughter, also Alice, was born in 1953.

Horses were an important part of farming at Rose Hill and Arthur and Jim became well known for their shire horses. In 1958 Richardson Bros., purchased 'Sanderling Rose' a show standard shire mare from which was bred

Hay time at Rose Hill Farm, Wharles. Arthur Richardson and mowing team about 1950.

several notable foals. Outstanding among their many horses was *'Rose Hill Twighlight'* born in 1966 and which won many trophies including the *Gold Champion Foal Cup at the Derby* Foal Stakes. This fine horse was sold to the Shire Horse Company of Canada as a five year old for the record price of £1000. Of course all the farming tasks were carried out by horse power until the first grey Ferguson tractor was purchased in 1960 although horses have never been fully eclipsed at Rose Hill.

Arthur died in 1982 following a long illness, when his daughter, Alice, and her mother worked the farm jointly without additional help. Alice herself became the tenant of Rose Hill in 1984, but had to appear before an Agricultural Tribunal to secure her tenancy and in the same year married Gordon Foster of Barnacre, Garstang. Alice and Gordon have a son, Matthew Richardson-Foster who was born in 1990. It was Alice who recalled the almost regimental regimes followed on the farm during her childhood, especially the domestic routines of the household:

Harvest at Wharles about 1940.

*'Monday was always washing day in the outbuildings with dolly tub, mangle and 'Dolly Blue' for boiling white clothes'*, which she remembered stained her fingers bright mauve blue (she hadn't, however, ever seen the Dolly Blue factory at Backbarrow on the Newby Bridge to Barrow Road in the Southern Lake District, where the whole countryside around the factory was stained blue). Water for washing was heated in a boiler by coal fire and she recalled some days when condensation would drip from the metal roof of the outhouse, while on frosty mornings the clothes would be frozen stiff. The ironing had to be completed the same day.

Tuesdays was a baking day and butter would be churned as well. It seemed that this was also the favourite day for tradesmen to call, Mr. Salisbury of the Co-op brought groceries; John Benson meat; and Mr. Woods the hardware man brought a variety of goods, from shoe polish to paraffin.

Wednesdays began with cleaning, then mending clothes, darning holes in stockings, before leaving for Preston for essential shopping.

Thursday was also baking day, but Friday was always bedroom cleaning day. Saturday's chores centred on cleaning all the windows in the house and swilling and scrubbing all the concrete paths round the property. Sunday was a day of rest with only essential housework being performed, but Alice remembered that her mother would always clean the family car, inside and out.

Of course, the farming chores never ceased. The Richardson cows were all tied in shippons for milking. They used six units, the milk being strained into ten gallon kits. The cows were fed *'cattle ration'* with hay, cabbage and turnips as added supplement in winter. The hens had a damp mash and the pigs were fed wet pig meal. Most seasonal farm work such as hedging and dyking, was done by hand, using traditional tools, but all hedge clippings were collected by horse and cart and formed the basis of the family's November 5th bonfire celebrations.

Since taking over the farm from her father, Alice has followed a family tradition by breeding and rearing horses, but has concentrated not on heavy work horses but on horses for hunting.

### Shorrocks Farm, Wharles

James and Ann Shorrock took over Shorrocks Farm in the 1850s, where they raised five sons and four daughters. This was one of the largest mixed farms in Wharles at that time. James was succeeded by his youngest son William and his wife Alice (nee Swift). They had five sons and one daughter.

Unfortunately William met with a tragic accident in September 1895, when early one evening he set out with his dog to check his stock. The dog came home, but William failed to return. His body was found in a deep pit on the farm. The inquest concluded that he had tripped in one of the many rabbit holes and fallen head first into the pit. As he was unable to swim, he drowned. He was 49. The farm was then taken over by two of his sons, James and Richard who farmed in partnership.

During world war two Shorrocks Farmhouse was used by the Royal Navy as a billet for Wren Officers from *HMS Nightjar*. (Wrens were the female members of the Royal Navy and its aeronautical branch, the Fleet Air Arm). Hundreds of sailors and wrens were based at Inskip, members of the Fleet Air Arm. Once a month they marched to Church in a formal parade.

The original farmhouse was situated in Ladies Row. There were two other cottages, one tied to New Hall Farm, the other to Isaac Ball's business.

In the 1950s Shorrocks was taken over by Joyce and Robert Stuart and their 3 children. They remained there with their two sons, Robert and David until the 1980s. Robert and his wife moved away to farm in South

Jimmy Shorrock of Shorrocks Farm, Wharles, in old age.

Wales, and have since emigrated to New Zealand. David has moved to a dairy farm in Yorkshire.

After the war many displaced persons from Europe were housed at Inskip camp. There was a Padre and his sons who would help out with Church services at a Chapel based at Four Oaks. There was also a Polish boy named Poly Joe, who is remembered with great affection by Joyce and Robert.

Shorrocks Farm is now the home of George and Jean Carter, who recounted a most unusual tale:

One night Jean was in the newly converted 'en-suite' bathroom, which had been built over an unused and now demolished staircase. In the bright electric light she clearly saw a man wearing a felt hat and old fashioned clothes emerge slowly through the floor, as though walking up the stairs that had once been there. He appeared to be as solid as you or I, yet he walked up to and then through poor Jean. This ghostly apparition was encountered on the night of the harvest moon.

### Stanley Grange Farm, (Off Dagger Road) Treales

It is believed that the Clarkson family helped to build Stanley Grange. They were followed by the Baldwin family. In 1933 the tenancy was taken by Cuthbert and Annie Fare, the farm then being 116 acres. They had 7 children, 6 boys and 1 girl. Their herd was dairy shorthorns, and horses were used on the farm. Cuthbert, however, invested in his first tractor in 1948.

On shooting day on the Estate the guns would gather at Stanley Grange at lunchtime and Annie would serve food. Lord Derby would sometimes attend the shoot.

Of their sons, Jack worked at Salwick Hall with race horses, while Tom worked at home. Tom married Edith in 1938 and they lived at Rose Cottage, which was without a water supply. They had to go next door to get water from the well at School House in order to do the washing. Tom would also bring water home from the farm.

Cuthbert died in 1954, but Annie carried on until 1958, when Tom and Edith moved to the farm with their three children, Tom, Peter and Anne. They had an Ayrshire herd and always milked in shippons. They were one of the first in the area to buy a bulk tank for the milk.

In 1971 Peter left the farm and took the tenancy of Post Farm, Roseacre, because it was felt that Stanley Grange would not be a viable farm once the M55 went through. His other son, Tom, now has a pig farm at Wrea Green.

Tom finally retired in 1986, and he and Edith moved to Kirkham. The land was divided between neighbouring farms and the house and buildings were sold to Andrew and Lise Southwood who moved in with their three children.

## Stanley Farm, Roseacre

John Shorrock took over the tenancy of Stanley Farm in the early 1900s. He was the son of William from Shorrocks Farm and was married to Elizabeth Marquis from Ash Tree Farm. They had one son and three daughters. It was a mixed farm, as were most of the farms in the area.

The cereal crops were harvested by a binder harvester into sheaves which were stooked in the fields to dry before being stored in the dutch barn until threshing day. The thresher, from Isaac Ball, Wharles, driven by a huge steam engine, went around the farms during the winter, threshing the grain from the sheaves. Labour was pooled from neighbouring farms and threshing days were a real community effort.

The milk from the dairy was used to make Lancashire cheese the best of which was shown at local shows. John and Elizabeth won many prizes including the Championship Silver Cup at the Preston Show. They won it outright after having won it three years in a row.

Their son William married Emily Pickervance from Roseacre Hall Farm in 1934 and they took over the tenancy of Stanley Farm. Emily remembers arriving in Roseacre as a small child in a milk kit (churn) with her brother Jack, a practical way of keeping them safe!

During the Second World War when *HMS Nightjar* was a Fleet Air Arm base, Stanley Farm was found to be in the flight path of the main runway. As a result the extensive orchard was felled and a red beacon placed on the roof of the house. Many a hen was startled into laying a premature egg in those days.

William and Emily had one daughter, Marguerite, and they continued to farm until they retired in the 1960s when they moved to Catforth. In 1968 David, the third son of John Pickervance of Roseacre Hall Farm married Joyce Critchley of Mythop Grange Farm near Blackpool. He continued to work for his father until 1975 when he built a pig unit at Stanley Grange, where he eventually had 220 sows and 2000 fatteners.

David and Joyce have four children, Jayne, Robert, Daniel and Richard who all attended Treales School even after they were given the tenancy of Mowbreck Hall Farm in 1982.

Stan Leeming lived at Stanley Farm between 1982 and 1986.

## Stud Farm, Blue Moor, off Church Road

Harry and Muriel Clark moved to Treales in 1921, walking all their stock from the railway station at Wesham, where they had arrived from Claugh House Farm (a Lord Derby property) Derbyshire. They lived at Ash Tree Farm for a short time and moved to Stud Farm in 1922. They took the tenancy over from the Butler family, the farm being in quite a

Heber Clark of Stud Farm, Treales, c1992.

poor state of repair. There was no mains water, electricity didn't arrive until 1939.

They had 6 children; Madge who married John Cowburn of Stanley Lodge Farm, Treales; Richard who became a joiner and lived at Singleton; Henry, died in infancy; Muriel who lived in Gloucestershire for many years before moving back to Kirkham, Edward, who married Annie Townsend of Kirkham who lived and farmed in Gloucestershire; and Heber, who married Margaret Haydock of Lea. All attended Treales School. Heber, would walk cows to the auction at Preston and then bike all the way back in time for school.

Harry died when he was 50, leaving Heber to continue farming with his mother. Later Heber and his wife, Margaret, ran the farm, which was 102 acres, with their four children. They had a pedigree herd of Ayrshire cows, prefix 'Blue Moor', and they were one of the first to have sheep in the area. They kept hens on a 'hatchability' scheme and eggs were also sold at the farm gate.

During the war they took lodgers from Inskip camp and one French couple who stayed for 3 months had their baby born at Stud Farm. Of their several workmen, one was Jack Platt from Roseacre, another Bill Blackburn of Rock Cottage, who was also the local gravedigger.

Heber and Margaret retired to Rose Cottage on Church Road in 1991, when Stud Farm was sold. The buildings, converted into 6 private residences are now known as Meadow Court. Heber was a pillar of the community; serving on the Parish Council for 30 years and a church warden for 22 years. He died in the garden of Rose Cottage in 1996. The

'Coopers Corner', Treales about 1900.

TREALES

name Stud Farm is self-explanatory, Lord Derby kept his stud horses there. The houses on the estate have traditionally been painted black and white because they were the Derby's racing colours.

Muriel Clark said that the estate installed a wind-pump to pump water to the farm from the pit at the bottom of the orchard in 1928, but that it ran dry in the first year. They then moved it to a pit under Brook Wood and thus secured a water supply to the water bowls in the Stud Farm Shippons.

The farm employed *'teamsmen'* who handled the horse-teams for ploughing. One, Will Saville, worked for them before the Second World War; another Fred Timms bought a motorised lorry for £100 and founded the *'Fred Timms Transport Company'*.

### White Carr Farm, Treales

The Cowell family moved to White Carr Farm in 1926, taking over from Ralph Platt and his family who moved to School House Farm. The Cowells originally came from Scorton. The farm was approximately 190 acres, with mainly hens and chickens, but also a few milk cows. They sold 1500 eggs a week. They used to take water and provin down the fields on a horse and cart for the hens.

During the war there were Land Girls at the farm and Prisoners of War, who walked from Kirkham. They grew mangels (large turnips) and these had to be pulled by hand. The labourers worked on their hands and knees and tied sacks to their knees to protect them. There were never less than 12 mouths to feed at meal times.

Tom Cowell took over the farm when his father retired in 1959. Tom decided to increase the milking herd and initially bought non-pedigree stock. In 1971, however, he built a new milking parlour and bought 6 pedigree Friesians from Singleton and 6 pedigree Holsteins from Leeds. The Holsteins averaged 4 gallons a day more milk, so he decided that in future he would have all Holsteins. John Slack from Wharles was one time herdsman, and David Noblett is the current holder of that post. Albert Hall also helps to run the farm. Tom has also bought in a few embryos from Canada. Many of his cows have won prizes at local shows. His prefix is 'White Carr'.

During the early 1990s Tom met Barbara. They travelled the world together. Sadly Barbara lost her battle against cancer in February 2000 and she will be missed by her family and friends.

### White Hall Farm, Treales

White Hall Farm was once the headquarters of a cattle feed business owned and run by Mr. Milner, a corn merchant. The following was quoted in the Preston Guardian, dated February 23rd 1895.

*"In the village, of which there appeared to be much dilapidated property, especially amongst the thatched cottages. The mill was at work grinding and not far away was a well stacked grain stackyard. Coming to Mr. Milner I was shown a Garnet mare which was in foal to 'Orchard Prince' and a light mare by 'Old Retainer' in foal to 'Dr. Fred'.*
*Mr. Milner does not keep many cattle and none of them have as yet dropped*

Cross Lane Farm, Treales. The man carrying the buckets is thought to be Harry Wright. The photo was taken around 1950.

The Marquis Family of Ash Tree Farm about 1900.

Rhododendron Cottage as restored in the 1980s.

photograph of 1925. There was a large family, but at the time of the photograph she had a son and his wife living with her and her daughter Ivy.

### Suddell family

The Suddell family farmed Cross Hill before Richardsons. They had 3 daughters and a son Harry. The son Harry lived in Rose Cottage with his wife. He sadly died in a pit at the rear of the cottage. One of the daughters married a Mr. Barton from Myerscough, a member of the Ayrshire Cattle Society, who became friends of Heber and Margaret Clark through the Club.

### Wards of Rhododendron Cottage

Harry Ward was a butcher and he butchered meat at Rhododendron Cottage. His son Harry lived at Ivy Dene and he was a pig butcher. They slaughtered the animals there and sold the meat from a horse and cart. The cottage was beautifully renovated in the 1980s by John and Janina Welch who still live there. It is one of the few remaining thatched cottages in the parish.

### The Wright family

The Wright family had a smallholding on Cross Lane and they kept poultry and grew raspberries to sell. Mrs Wright lost her husband and eldest daughter to TB, and their son Harry was not well, having to leave school in the winter months because of chest problems. The original cottage was thatched, but was replaced in the same place with the bungalow, which is there now. Harry and his wife Kitty farmed there until their retirement in the early 1970s.

### The Young Farmers Club

Although the parish cannot boast a Young Farmers Club of its own, many young people, especially those living on local farms are active members of the Kirkham branch of the club.

Membership is both educational and social but with emphasis being placed on activities associated with farming. Thus members have the opportunity of participating in farm visits, stock judging, lectures, and competitions based on farming skills, e.g. ploughing. Many of the clubs social events revolve around fundraising for charity, which is seen as one of their most important activities. Each year the local branch entertain underprivileged children, providing a trip to a pantomime, followed by a party held at Newton Village Hall. They are innovative in their fundraising

*any calves, although several are nearly due. Among the numerous Berkshire Tamworth and white pigs five are in pig".*

White Hall was later farmed by the Cooper family, but its buildings are now subject to planning consent to be converted into housing. The Coopers have retained the farmhouse but with a greatly reduced acreage.

### Other Properties

In earlier years many houses had crofts and a small number of fields and could claim to be small farms. Treales Road and Kirkham Road were lined with small farms:- Derby Farm, Hill Farm, Ash Cottage Farm, Stanley Farm, Johnsons Farm and Smithy, and Primrose Farm .

However, many other properties are now private residences, or tied cottages:- Windmill Farm, Heights Farm, Cardwells Farm, The Derby Arms and the Eagle and Child, both of which were small farms. Saswick Farm last tenanted by the Molloys was sold and the buildings converted. Stanley Farm, was incorporated into Roseacre Hall Farm. Moorside Farm (West View Farm) is a private residence. Cross Lane Farm, last worked by Harry & Kitty Wright lost its land when the Wrights retired. Harry and Kitty remained in the farmhouse. Boundary Farm and Roseacre Farm are now private residences.

### Jennison family

The Jennison family lived in Butts Lane and Mrs Jennison was a widow. There were no state benefits and she could only live on what could be grown on their smallholding. The youngest of the family, Ivy, is in the school techniques; profit from their social evening, selling manure for gardens, to carol singing. Not very long ago they raised money by cycling to Torquay, not on conventional bicycles, but on a *'Wot Not'* a specially fabricated four wheel machine. In the year 2000 their aim is to provide a dog for a profoundly deaf person.

### The sale of the Fylde Estate by the Church Commissioners

In 1971 the Fylde Estate was offered for sale. The sale particulars, published by Smith Gore, chartered surveyors, listed the 22 working farms remaining in the Parish. Below is shown a 'then and now' table of the properties for sale:

*Farm, Occupier, area & rent paid 1971, Use in Year 2000*

| New Hall Farm | G. Carter | 379 acres | £3790.00 |
|---|---|---|---|
| Farmed by Mr. Barnes of Bashall, Eaves | | | |
| Stud Farm | H. Clark | 120 acres | £975.00 |
| Converted into 7 private residences | | | |
| Ash Tree Farm | H. Cookson | 142 acres | £1,160.00 |
| Private Residence | | | |
| Heights Farm | J.J. Richardson | 46 acres | £450.00 |
| 2 Private Residences | | | |
| White Hall Farm | L.H. Cooper | 182 acres | £1480.00 |
| Buildings planning consent for conversion and some land retained by J & E Cooper | | | |
| Stanley Lodge Farm | W. J. Towers | 215 acres | £2000.00 |
| Amalgamated with Hale Hall Farm, D & D Hall. | | | |
| White Carr Farm | T. Cowell | 267 acres | £2100.00 |
| Farmed by T. Cowell | | | |
| Stanley Grange Farm | T. Fare | 116 acres | £1050.00 |
| Private residence & stables A. & L. Southwood | | | |
| Hale Hall Farm | P. W. Hall | 206 acres | £1700.00 |
| Farmed by Hall Bros. | | | |
| Cardwell Farm | J. Hesketh | 127 acres | £1080.00 |
| Private residence and building converted into houses. | | | |
| Moss House Farm | G. R. Hogarth | 196 acres | £2000.00 |
| Farmed by J. & G. Gardner | | | |
| Smithy land | J. B. Johnson | 36 acres | £240.00 |
| Farmed by J. Johnson | | | |
| Grange Farm | J. Melling | 308 acres | £3000.00 |
| Farmed by O. & H. Melling | | | |
| Saswick House Farm | T. Molloy | 142 acres | £1180.00 |
| Private residence & buildings converted into 5 houses. | | | |
| Post Farm | P. Fare | 86 acres | £900.00 |
| Farmed by P. & P. Fare | | | |
| Southview Farm | J. Parkinson | 93 acres | £920.00 |
| Farmed by R & G. Baxter | | | |
| Land, Old School House | R. Platt | 31 acres | £275.00 |
| 2 Private Residence | | | |
| Roseacre Hall Farm | J. Pickervance | 256 acres | £2468.00 |
| Farmed by H. & C. Pickervance | | | |
| Cross Hill Farm | W. Robinson | 180 acres | £1758.00 |
| Farmed by B. W. & J. Robinson | | | |
| Rose Hill Farm | A. Richardson | 74 acres | £730.00 |
| Farmed by G. & A. Richardson-Foster | | | |
| Mee Farm | J. Sanderson | 94 acres | £960.00 |
| Farmed by A. & S.M. Sanderson | | | |
| Derby Lodge Farm | G. M. Towers | 241 acres | £2000.00 |
| Farmed by J. & G. Thornley | | | |

In the year 2000 only 14 working farms exist. One new farm, Church View, has been created, worked by W. & K. Salisbury.

### The Heskeths of Cardwells Farm

Of all the families of the parish, the Heskeths have one of the most fascinating histories. Evidence for this claim is recorded in the Hesketh Family Bible, now in the possession of Elizabeth Jenkinson (née Hesketh), which dates from 1815 until the present day. However, as interesting as this is, the family's earlier recorded history lends more to heraldry than markings in a Bible. Elizabeth inherited the Hesketh family tree from Jeanetta Coxhead, (her grandmother' sister) on Jeanetta's demise. This traced the family directly to the Heskeths of Rufford, and from that point no further research was necessary as it was already written and proved in several reputable histories of Lancashire. Earlier research by the family had led to the name *George Hesketh*, who had married in the early 1600s, *'Jane, widow of Sherbourne, younger brother of 'Sherbourne of Stoneyhurst'.'* * (See *History of the County Palatine & Duchy of Lancaster*, James Croston, 1891, Volume IV. Pedigree: Hesketh of Hesketh & Rufford, pages 155-7).

George Hesketh was the son of Robert Heskaith, *'Lord of Heskaith, Rufford, Holmes and Holmwood, Martholme, Great Harwood. Hongwick and Beckonsaile: had warranty for livery on his father's land'. 19th May, 31st year of Elizabeth I's reign, 1584.* He was also Member of Parliament for Lancashire 1597-98. However, perhaps of greater interest to the parish is that his mother was *'Mary, daughter and heir of Sir George Stanley, Knight, Marshall of Ireland and Captain of the Isle of Man (the grandson of George, Lord Strange of Knockyn, eldest son of the first Earl of Derby).'* This pedigree proves that not only are the Heskeths descended directly from the first Earl of Derby, but also can trace their lineage earlier to 1298, when Willyam de Heskayth married Annabilla Stafford, and to the ultimate founder of the Hesketh dynasty Richard de Heskaythe in the late 1100s.

The first Heskeths came to Treales in 1880 from Tarleton at the express wish of Lord Derby, who granted them the tenancy of his farm, Derby Lodge, at Roseacre. According to the family archives Robert and Sarah Anne Hesketh (nee Parkinson, born at Salwick) were the first large farm tenants on the Derby Fylde Estate and this was given because of the relationship existing between the Heskeths and the Derbys.

Four children were born at Roseacre, John born September 2$^{nd}$ 1883 (was to move to Cardwells) Richard, the well known owner of Treales Garage, Robert who lived at the Cross Keys, Whitechapel, and Elizabeth who married a Fisher from St. Michael's on Wyre.

However, tragedy was to strike this family, Robert and Sarah Ann both died while their children were still young. Orphans, three of the children were brought up by Richard Hesketh, Robert's brother, then resident at Moorside Farm, Treales. The children remaining in Treales were John, Richard and Betty (Elizabeth), Robert being fostered on his mother's side by the Parkinsons.

John was to marry Ellen Ball, daughter of Isaac Ball, of Banks, Nr. Southport, later of Wharles, and of steam engine fame, and lived for a short while at Rhododendron Cottage, Treales. While living there the couple were offered the vacant and run down farming property, Cardwells Farm, on Treales Road. Because of its poor state, (the farmhouse was old and in disrepair and the land neglected) the Derby offer was that they could have the tenancy free for the first twelve months and that a new farmhouse would be built. This they accepted and Cardwells Farmhouse was built specially for them.

John and Ellen Hesketh had five children born at Cardwells; Sarah-Annie, John, Jenny, Robert and Nellie. They were to farm together at Cardwells until John's death in January 1937. The line of succession then allowed his second child, John, born on May 13$^{th}$, 1912, to take the joint tenancy with his mother Ellen. He was to remain at Cardwells for the whole of his seventy five years. John married Annie Fare of Yewtree Farm, Salwick, on April 29$^{th}$ 1948 and they had two children, Elizabeth and John. He took over the tenancy in his own right and farmed Cardwells until his death in 1987. This was a mixed farm run on traditional lines. It was an easily managed farm, its fields adjacent to the farmhouse and mainly interconnected. Initially the motive power was the horse and John followed in his fathers footsteps in his love of heavy horses, but inevitably the tractor replaced the Shire and the role of the tractor driver was taken over by his son, John. His daughter Elizabeth shared milking and young stock rearing, while Mrs. Hesketh raised poultry, up to five hundred turkeys, hens and guinea fowl as well as her duties associated with the farmhouse. As happened with other farms (following the sale of the estate by the Church Commissioners) when John Hesketh died in 1987 the tenancy died with him and the remaining family, Annie and her son, John were given no option but to move out, the farmland being amalgamated with other farms and the farmhouse and buildings put up for sale.

### Cardwells in the 1950s as remembered by Elizabeth Jenkinson

Cardwells from the 1950s onwards is remembered with great affection by Elizabeth. Still in her possession is a cloth map of the farm showing the individual fields and acreages and these were all known by name. In the back field behind the farm was the quaintly named Mackerel field, their smallest this side of the railway, being just 2$^{1}/_{2}$ acres. This she remembers was so called because a Miss Mackerel had a small cottage and croft in that position. She also recalled seeing Cardwells described on an early map as Halls House and wondered why this should have been, it being Cardwells on earlier and later maps? She said that some of the fields, especially Kelly's Nook, with its steep bank running towards the railway always appeared hazardous. The slope was so great that tractors always felt as though they would roll over if traversing the slope and this feeling was compounded when a heavy steam train thundered by, often engulfing the tractor in black smoke. She recalled that it was most exciting the night that the signal box caught fire!

She had, like most who feel close to their land, a particular favourite pasture; 'old Annies' (now covered over with the gas terminal in Jacob's Lane) they acquired on the death of Annie Benson who had lived opposite Treales Garage. This was a meadow never ploughed, with feathered grasses of multiple colours, pink, blues and purples making hay with a perfume chemistry cannot imitate. Another favourite, only one and a half acres lay over the railway bridge and beyond over Spen Brook, reached via a wooden sleeper bridge hardly wide enough to take the grey Ferguson tractor and binder. This was a cornfield and she enthused as she thought of the balmy autumnal afternoons stacking sheaves into stooks.

Animals too loom large in her memory. *Old Betty* (which they aptly named after their Aunt Betty) was the first pedigree Friesian bought by her father in the early fifties and a friend and trusted servant of the family for over twenty years. That they nursed this cow (in what was to be unfortunately her last illness) for six nights in a valiant attempt to save her life says much for the empathy that many of the older families had with their animals.

Richard Hesketh of Treales Garage with early motor car. The invoice is interesting, pool petrol only being sold during World Ward II.

Tel: KIRKHAM 78.     1392

TREALES, NR. KIRKHAM.

Mr J. Melling
Treales        Dec 30th 1939

## DR. TO RICHARD HESKETH.
### MOTOR ENGINEER.
#### AUTHORISED FORD DEALER.

VACUUM OILS.    GARAGE.    REPAIRS.    HIRING.    B.S.A. and TRIUMPH MOTORS.

Customers' Cars are only Driven by our Staff at Customers' own Risk and Responsibility.

| 1939 | | | | | | | |
|---|---|---|---|---|---|---|---|
| Aug. | | | B F | £ | 7 - 9 - 11 | | |
| 11" | To 4 gallons of HT | @ | 1/7 | | 6 - 4 | | |
| 17" | 4 | | | | 6 - 4 | | |
| Sept 4" | 5 | | | | 7 - 11 | | |
| 13" | 2 quarts Vac B B | | | | 3 - 8 | | |
| 13" | 3 gallons of HT | 1/7 | | | 4 - 9 | | |
| Oct 2nd | 3 | Pool Petrol | 1/6 | | 4 - 6 | | |
| 5" | 4 | | | | 6 - 0 | | |
| 13" | 4 | | | | 6 - 0 | | |
| 18" | 2 | | | 1/8 | 3 - 4 | | |
| 24" | 5 | | | 1/8 | 8 - 4 | | |
| Nov 6" | 4 | | | | 6 - 8 | | |
| 11" | 3 | | | | 5 - 0 | | |
| 21" | 4 | | | 1/9½ | 7 - 2 | | |
| 28" | 3 | | | 1/9½ | 5 - 4½ | | |
| Dec 2nd | 2 | | | | 3 - 7 | | |
| 5" | 3 | | | | 5 - 4½ | | |
| 16" | 4 | | | | 7 - 2 | | |
| | | | | £ | 12 - 7 - 5 | | |

£12-7-5

Their Hereford bull *Rufus* also deserved special mention. Elizabeth remembers him, standing underneath the hawthorn tree in their croft for hours, day dreaming and gently scratching his back. At milking time he would come home with his cows and stand placidly at the back of the shippon until the cows, each in their own stall, would be released back to pasture, when he would trundle off with them. Their dogs, *Laddie* and *Lady*, both Border Collies slept in the house behind the scroll arm settee, but Fly, almost too enthusiastic, slept in his kennel. He had distinctive eyes, odd coloured and known to the family as *'woe-eyed'*.

Cardwells always boasted a flock of guinea fowl, hyper-sensitive birds which are probably better guards than geese, certainly alert to any strangers as they roosted in the Sycamore tree in the back garden. Turkeys were the responsibility of her mother, and she remembered supplying them for Christmas as far afield as Hoghton to Sir Bernard de Hoghton of Hoghton Towers.

They were 'avant garde' in some ways, experimenting with soothing music in their shippons to test a current theory that contented *'musically educated'* herds would produce greater milk yields, but she has her doubts as to whether this achieved the desired result. Elizabeth's special role on the farm was the rearing of calves and young stock and she has an enviable reputation for her skill in this taxing job. She also recalled the visits of the veterinary surgeon, for testing purposes, and attending to sick animals. Tubercular Testing was always a nightmare, but the vet, Jackie Kidd, always coped with whatever emergency. She remembers him saying to her in her late teens that she was the first milkmaid that he had ever seen with pink varnished toe nails, and this seemed to evoke particular happy memories of her youth, and more carefree days as she coped with everyday farm life. The trauma of her father's untimely death and the behaviour of the Land Agents then administering the estate in closing down the farm is a memory that will never leave her. Told that there was *'no sentiment in commerce'*, they were asked to leave Cardwells almost at a minutes notice and this denial of their chosen way of life has left them scarred and bitter.

It was a sad and uncalled for end to a good farm, and the dispersal of a well-respected family.

## Richard (Dick) Hesketh, Agricultural Engineer

Of the four orphaned children of Robert and Sarah Anne Hesketh, perhaps Dick Hesketh has received most publicity if not notoriety. He was certainly an entrepreneur and businessman and made a considerable amount of money through his association with mechanised farming. However, it might be argued that he owed his good fortune to John, who allowed his brother to start a business from cabins erected in the stack yard of Cardwells farm, where Treales Garage stands today.

It was here that he co-operated during the First World War with the Ministry of Agriculture and engineered ploughing devices using steam engines and cables which drew the plough from end to end of the field. He was also fanatically interested in motor cars and owned, and is said to have raced, several makes of early automobiles. He developed the garage at Treales as it is today and during his tenancy the first petrol pumps were installed. Lord Derby disliked the visual appearance of the early petrol pumps, which were hand cranked, and insisted that those installed at Treales were enclosed in a lockable cupboard when not in use. These same pumps were still in existence into the 1960s when they were changed for non-mechanical versions.

Richard Hesketh expanded his business by opening another garage complex near to the Shard Bridge by Skippool and although he visited Cardwells every week, he built a large house near to his new garage and lived there until his death. He also lived for a period of time while he was developing Treales Garage at the now Deer Leap Cottage on Treales Road opposite the garage.

He married Annie, a daughter of Isaac Ball, and had one daughter who never married. In recent years, Treales Garage has been owned by Dave Sumner.

## Robert Ball Hesketh - War Hero

Robert Ball Hesketh was the fourth of five children born to John and Ellen (nee Ball) Hesketh at Cardwells Farm. He was born in 1919 and died in 1993 aged 74 years.

He attended Treales School and later Kirkham Grammar School. When he left school he joined the Midland Bank rather than follow his father into farming, but at the outbreak of war in 1939 enlisted in the Herefordshire Regiment and saw active service in France early in 1940. He served initially as a non-commissioned officer but rose through the ranks to hold a commission and when he left the army in 1945 held the rank of Major.

He was serving with the Herefordshire Regiment in France at the withdrawal of the Expeditionary Force at Dunkirk. He was a member of the D-Day liberation Army in 1944 and received the Military Cross for bravery under fire.

The War Office citation held by his family confirms that as Acting Captain attached to the 1st Battalion, The Herefordshire Regiment, 11th Armoured Division, he landed on June 13th 1944 (with the D-Day landing forces):

*"…and served continuously throughout the campaign. Initially he was Radio Signal Officer and did invaluable work ensuring that the communications upon which life of the Battalion depend, kept going even under the most difficult conditions. He received facial injuries on the 30th July 1944 at Cajmont, but insisted in not being evacuated beyond the field ambulance post, and after the minimum period forced his way up to the Battalion. He was appointed Adjutant in August 1944, since when he has carried out his duties with the utmost keenness and efficiency. He has always been at Tactical Battalion Headquarters and therefore frequently under intensive artillery and mortar fire. However unpleasant the situation, and however tired through lack of sleep he has always displayed a coolness which inspired the confidence of the Company Commanders, to whom he was responsible for giving the C.O's orders.*
*At times during the battle he was the only Officer at Battalion Headquarters and his tactical ability coupled with his determination to see that his Commanding Officer's intention was carried out, ensured that he could be relied upon to make the right decision".*

This document was countersigned confirming his recommendation to receive the Military Cross by Major Peter Crofts, 1st Herefordshire Regiment, Brigadier J.B. Churcher, DSC., Commander 159 Infantry Brigade, the Major General commanding 11th Armoured Division (signature unreadable) and the Lieutenant General Commanding 8 Corps. (signature unreadable). His Military Cross was placed on his flag-draped coffin at his funeral and is now held by his son.

Following the war he returned to banking, being promoted through the Midland Bank system to become a director of the bank. He retired to live in Sheffield, Yorkshire, where he died on the 2nd of April 1993.

## GAMEKEEPING IN THE PARISH

That the countryside is as it is today has depended on man's manipulation of nature rather than on nature itself. The landscape within the parish has changed and fluctuated with farming fashions. Many changes have occurred within the life span of most living in the parish now. Parish boundaries have always been set by physical features, roads, pathways, streams, woodland, etc., but what has happened in between is largely due to those altering the terrain for their own convenience.

The parish is well served with covert-type woodland, mostly planted by the Earls of Derby in the late 1800s, and maintained by estate workers and game keepers mainly for the protection and production of game. That these woods form the character of our Fylde landscape is an incidental bonus, but one which brings considerable pleasure to resident and visitor alike. In the early days of the Derby Estate game was largely self-

Mr. Kenyon, Head Game Keeper, with Matt Roskell, c1925.

perpetuating. It was not until much later in the twentieth century that the mass rearing of artificial numbers of game birds became the norm. In many ways this came about by changes in agricultural practice.

The earlier leisurely, labour intensive, horse-drawn era, with rough pasture, winter stubble, hay made later in the year's calendar than modern day silage, allowed for wild life to regroup and regenerate alongside man's activity.

There was time for the hare to make its form and produce its young in hay fields before the grass was cut. Similarly birds such as the plover and skylark could rear their young before whichever crop was harvested. Few, if any, sprays were used, machinery moved at a leisurely pace, giving time for a man mowing with a horse drawn machine to move a plover's nest rather than smash it, (eggs or chicks) with the mower. This was an era of farmer/gamekeeper liaison, one depending on the other, respect and co-operation a common aim. These too, were the great days of game and the time of the gentleman gamekeeper. Mr. Kenyon, from the Derby seat at Knowsley was installed at Treales Cottage, situated in the field off Treales Road, as Head Gamekeeper. Centred on Mowbreck Hall, the Derby shooting parties would 'shoot' the Fylde Estate, often stopping at Treales Cottage to lunch, the meals being prepared for many titled guests by Mrs. Kenyon.

Unfortunately there are now no known existing records of game shot until 1943. Joan Trippier, Mr. Kenyon's daughter, still has her father's game-book for the years 1943 - 1949 – a specially designed hard-backed ledger, meticulously kept by the Head Keeper, and giving such details as the ground shot over, the guns named, game killed by species, and how these animals were disposed of. This book reads like a Who's Who, but most interesting are the totals of animals killed, which would indicate that this was a land teeming with wild life.

In the year February 1943 until February, 1944, one thousand, five hundred and fifty eight rabbits were shot, with relatively few game birds, eighty seven pheasants, fifty wild duck, fifty three partridge, but one hundred and seventy one hares. In that same year many tenants and estate servants in the parish benefited greatly from this slaughter. J. Cowell was listed as receiving 441 rabbits, Mrs. Towers 47 rabbits, A Pickervance 128 rabbits, while Mowbreck Hall and its workmen received 372 rabbits. Taking one page at random from this ledger, November 17th 1948, the shooting party consisted of seven guns, amongst whom were Lord Derby, The Hon. Richard Stanley, Major Brett, and the Duke of Roxburgh. This party killed seventy-two pheasants, five partridge, fifty-five hares, eleven rabbits, one woodcock and five wild duck. In the year 1949 it is stated that

Mr. Armstrong, Under Keeper to Mr. Kenyon outside Middleton Cottage, Treales circa 1900. The black and white chequers on his stockings represent Lord Derby's racing colours.

Commissioners for England. They in turn appointed George Scott as Head Keeper, the shoot being let to Leyland Paints of Leyland. Mr. Scott lived at Melbourne House, Treales, as did his successor, John Elliot who had Alan Walker, Matthew Roskell's grandson, as his Under Keeper. Alan was soon to be promoted, moving to the Barnacre Shoot at Garstang as Head Keeper. However, in a change of syndicates, John Elliot moved to Barnacre as Head Keeper and Alan Walker returned to Treales as Head Keeper to Thomas Cowell who now rented the shoot. With the disposal of the estate to Mountleigh the shoot passed into private hands. The parish, neatly bisected by the M55 Motorway, allowed most of the land to the north of this highway to be leased by Cowell, the land to the south by Jim Harrison and Oliver Melling. Alan Walker remembers his grandfather, Matthew Roskell, with great affection:

*"He was born at Out Rawcliffe and initially went to work on a farm. However, aged sixteen, he got the opportunity to work as Under Keeper on the Weeton Estate, He received no salary, but was given free board and lodgings in the Head Keeper's cottage. He met his future wife, Edith, who lived in Wesham, and they married in 1912. Matthew served in the First World War, moving to Treales in 1920 when he was appointed Under Keeper to Mr. Kenyon. He was later appointed Head Keeper on the death of Mr. Kenyon. He was noted for his kindness and would rise at 4.00 am and go round Treales lighting fires in the homes of farmers, returning home for his breakfast around 10.00 am. In his later years he was appointed Keeper to the Salwick Estate, where he worked till just before his death of a stroke".*

### What of the future?

Alan, himself a lifelong shooter is nevertheless philosophical about the fate of his sport. He is a keen conservationist and has worked tirelessly for many years to bring closer ties between the 'gun-lobby' and those totally opposed to shooting. He has worked with *English Nature* and wildfowlers on the creation of sound management techniques for wildfowl on the River Ribble Estuary and is a keen believer in the need for positive management of habitats for wildlife. A true countryman he feels that there is no longer the bond between farmers and gamekeepers that existed in the days of the great estates. He thinks that elsewhere in the country shooting has become too commercial, farmers and landowners diversifying, producing as many

in the parish the tenants and estate workers were given a total of 535 rabbits. In the same year, Fred Crane (mentioned elsewhere) was given one hare for his services as driver of the horse and cart which accompanied the shoot and collected the animals shot. It is known that this cart was superbly painted and meticulously polished and the horse, specially trained to stand still despite the barrage of gunshot, was groomed and bedecked with brasses and ribbons to match the splendour of the cart.

The list of gamekeepers last century is suprisingly short, Mr. Kenyon serving as Head Keeper for almost half the century, aided by various Under-Keepers, Mr. Robinson, Mr. Armstrong, Matthew Roskell. The Estate at this time covered Weeton, Sowerby, Treales, Inskip, Wharles and Roseacre. On the death of Mr. Kenyon he was succeeded by Matthew Roskell who remained in the post until the estate was sold to the Church

Pencil drawing by Shirley Lee from the painting by the railway artist Hamilton Ellis. It shows Locomotive No. 290 *'ATKINSON'*, built at Miles Platting, Manchester, in 1861, heading the L & Y Railway's Manchester – Blackpool Express on Treales Roads, approaching Kirkham, Treales Windmill in the background.

game birds as possible, for a minority of rich guns to shoot. He is pessimistic as to whether the good traditions of the countryside will survive this commercialism. He has achieved considerable success in breeding and training labrador gun-dogs and travels regularly to game-fairs to judge gun dog classes, such is his interest in the sport. He notes that in this parish some farmers and owners of woodland are beginning to manage their woods to encourage natural regeneration and is pleased with the new woodland planting that is taking place. He is sure that this management is essential for all the older woodland within our area which must be nearing the end of its natural life. If this is done the Fylde countryside will remain as beautiful as it is today.

### THE RAILWAY – AN IMPACT ON THE VILLAGE

The Fylde was a most remote and desolate area in early history and this remained largely true until the advent of the railway which runs virtually alongside Spen brook which forms the southern boundary of the village.

That the area was served by rail was largely due to the vision of one man, Sir Peter Hesketh Fleetwood, politician, landowner, businessman and philanthropist, whose lasting memorial is his town, Fleetwood, on the Fylde coast. A deeply religious man he was a follower of the industrial reformer, Robert Owen, famous for his non-profit making revolutionary social experimentation in industrial relationships.

He realised however, that the establishment of competitive industry relies on good trade routes and communications. The main Fylde highway from Preston to the Fylde Coast was most unsuitable, almost impassable for most of the year whenever rain penetrated its rutted dirt surface. The

Mr. & Mrs. Crane and daughters, Hettie and Edith at South
View Cottage, Treales circa 1900.

Like many residents of the parish, Alice Ainscough, (Harry Hall's
aunt) worked in one of the several mills in Kirkham, c1920.

opening of the Clifton Turnpike in 1787 did improve travelling conditions, but it was obvious that the region would require a coastal shipping contact with the outside world if the growing industrial base was to prosper.

In 1834 plans to build a railway were inaugurated by a cohort of merchants and civic leaders including Hesketh Fleetwood, Thomas Birley of Kirkham and Hugh Hornby of Ribby who jointly published a prospectus for the Preston and Wyre Railway. Colonel George Landmann surveyed this on behalf of the proposers who suggested a route from Maudland Bank, Preston (by the University of Central Lancashire) passing through Lea, Salwick, Treales, Kirkham, Thornton, Burn Naze, and Fleetwood. The project received Royal Assent by Act of Parliament dated July 3rd 1835. Work commenced under the direction of George and Robert Stephenson of railway fame and opened in 1840.

By the time that the railway reached Fleetwood the population of Blackpool was in the region of 2000 people only. That the railway made an impact on the life of the parish through Kirkham and Salwick Stations is evident. The population of Treales, Wharles and Roseacre in the census following the opening of the railway was one third of that of Blackpool itself, a total of 696. It can be assumed that not all the population was engaged in agricultural employment and that many parish residents worked in the mills of Kirkham. The Birleys, who had a controlling interest in the Preston & Wyre railway, had almost a monopoly of the manufacture of sailcloth. This they manufactured under contract for the Admiralty and this together with their other principal commodity, linen, could now be distributed world-wide via the port of Fleetwood and the rapidly expanding national rail network. This brought great prosperity to these family owned enterprises until steam propulsion eclipsed the sailing ship.

The transport of farm produce via the railway stations at Kirkham and Salwick was a boon to the residents of the Parish, MacLaughlin in the book *'Railways of the Fylde'* quotes recollections of the early morning milk train and the *'Market Special'* which ran each Saturday morning to the markets of Preston. With the erection of cattle pens and goods sidings it was possible to transport cattle to markets in the large conurbations and to import new blood lines from distant herds. The tariffs for carrying passengers and freight for the early Preston & Wyre railway make interesting reading:

*'3d per mile for First Class passengers'*
*'2¹/₂d per mile for bulls, oxen, etc.'*
*'Lambs and small creatures 3 farthings per mile'*

More than one local farmer remembers carting coal and lime from the sidings at Salwick and Kirkham. Coal became an easily available fuel once the links were made with the Lancashire coalfield. Prior to the railway, import of coal had been via Freckleton on the Ribble and Wardleys and Skippool on the Wyre. Many a sheepdog from Wales, or calf (placed in a sack with only its head protruding and labelled to a forwarding address) was carried in the Guard's van of a train, to be collected by local farmers. Local research revealed at least three village families who were dependent upon the railway, these are accounts from relatives of those now long gone.

Late in the 1800s after leaving Treales School aged fourteen years, Thomas Parkinson who was later to farm at South View Farm, was employed as stable lad to the Clayton family of Moorfield Farm. The Claytons were a prosperous family with a large butchery business in Preston, and were well known for their stables of fine thoroughbred horses.

It was the duty of the stable-lad each morning to transport the working members of the Clayton family by horse and trap to Salwick Station to meet the Preston train. They were met on their return in the evening and taken back to Moorfield.

Alice Crane of South View Cottage caught the train each Saturday morning from Salwick Station to Preston with her basket of butter, produced from the one cow that the family kept on their croft. This family had additional links with the railway. Her husband, Tom Crane was employed as railway linesman responsible for the care of the line from Salwick Troughs, Treales Roads to Kirkham Station.

Likewise Jim Fisher of Windmill Farm, Treales, caught the same Saturday train to sell his produce on Preston Market. Grace Baxter who recalled these events also remembers Fred Crane carting lime to South View Farm from Kirkham Sidings.

Treales also had its own railway sidings situated at the one time Sidings Farm, now the home of the Boys' Brigade. Lime, fertiliser and coal were brought into the Parish from these sidings and it has been suggested that it was also linked to The Derby Brick Works. Goods destined for Mowbreck Hall were also brought via this siding, especially when the Derbys and their houseguests were resident there.

## TREALES WINDMILL — A SHORT HISTORY
### Introduction

The obvious source book for a history of windmills in the Fylde is *'Windmill Land'* by Allen Clarke, published in 1916.

Given the lack of easily obtainable historical records in the early 1900s it is hardly surprising that his six-page chapter on Treales Mill is lacking in detail. He describes the route to be taken to Treales village; indicates that the area, once in the hands of the Butler family, was now part of the Derby estate; and enthused that the Parish of Treales, Wharles, and Roseacre had *'plenty of room and unlimited fresh air'*. However, his description of Treales windmill is meagre:-

*"Treales Mill is in a green lane, close to the farmhouse where the miller lives. It is a tower mill four storeys high. The drying house (kiln) is a dozen yards away from the mill and is connected with a little stone causeway on a bank of earth a yard high. The date of the mill's erection is not known'.*

Clarke's enthusiastic descriptions of the Fylde countryside helped make the Fylde a mecca for tourists. Regular cycle and motor bus tours followed his prescribed routes in the early years of the twentieth century. His deep regard for the Fylde obviously stemmed from his childhood years. In his introductory chapter to *'Windmill Land'* he tells of his first sighting of a windmill.

*'The first windmill I ever saw was a Fylde mill, I was then a little tiny boy on a day excursion (to Blackpool 1875) with my father. I remember well the first joyous glimpse of the sea…but more profoundly do I remember the sight of the first windmill we saw from the train. It must have been the Treales mill between Preston and Kirkham. That first windmill, the picturesque white tower with red-brown wings (sails)\*…was a thrilling sight to me. It belonged to a world not of factories and smoke, but of Arcadian skies and Elysian fields, where all the days were poetry and all the nights romance'.*

Treales Windmill 1959 now derelict, showing the cedar shingle roof made by Rushton Bros., of Foundry Yard in 1938.

Treales Windmill 1900. Bede Cartmell can be seen standing between the mill and kiln.

*The sails of Fylde windmills were traditionally painted red-brown, the towers were whitewashed using limewash with the addition of animal-derived 'tallow' as a water-proofing agent. This would be applied by brush from trestles attached to the stationary sails, the cap being slowly rotated through 360°. There are no references to preservative treatments for the wooden caps. Tar was a traditional preservative in some parts of the country but this added to the fire risk. Presumably creosote was also available and widely used to preserve wood.

### Earlier Windmills

The tracing of individual buildings is difficult even when they were estate owned and thus more likely to be recorded in estate accounts and archives. Fortunately, most of the archive material relating to the Earls of Derby is held at the Lancashire Record Office in Preston. However, these can prove difficult to translate, and are not as exact as one would wish. An early Derby document dated *'April 22nd in the 37th year of Elizabeth I, A.D. 1595'* and relating to the *'Inquisition post-mortem taken after the death of Ferdinande, Earl of Derby in the County of Lancaster'* lists the family holdings at that date *'and also of and in 2000 messuages, 200 cottages, 20 mills'*. (a messuage is described in the Oxford Dictionary as a dwelling house with outbuildings and land assigned to its use).

'Trayles' is listed as one of the hamlets within the survey, but it is impossible to prove the existence of a windmill at Treales at that early date. Indeed, the earliest accurate reference found to describe a windmill is within a later Derby survey, *'Estates in the Filde, 1798-1801, by E. Oldman, Scriptor'*. Entry 118 of this document shows Treales windmill as a wooden post mill together with its kiln and mill field. There is some evidence that this wooden mill was constructed in 1718 but all that is known for certain is that this mill must have been working before the survey date of 1798. Also included is the named tenant of the mill:

*'Henry Barnes, Mill and Mill Stead, 1 pole, 1 perch, kiln, house and garden...also 1 acre of moss in Wharles'*.

It is almost certain that Henry Barnes was the son of James Barnes, both of whom appear with Henry's siblings in the *'1767 List of papists in the county of Lancaster at Greenall with Thistleton'*.

Henry Barnes is known to have died at Treales Mill in 1822, and is buried at the Willows Catholic cemetery in Kirkham.

It is probable that the 1718 date stone, which is built into the lower floor of the present brick mill, was taken from the wooden mill described above and incorporated into the current building as a mark of continuation. Certainly the present windmill stands on the site of the mill illustrated in the 1798 survey which must have been coming to the end of its useful life by that date.

### The present brick tower Mill

No document seems to be in existence which categorically dates the present structure, but it is almost certain that it was built in the first decade of the nineteenth century. The same miller, Henry Barnes, links this and the former mill as he was resident on site until his death, in 1822. Most of the bricks for Fylde estate buildings were hand crafted by Derby estate workers, the clay being dug from clay pits in the Parish. It is not known whether the mill was built by estate workers or by one of the specialist millwrights working within the Fylde area. (Perhaps the most well known local millwright was Ralph Slater, known to have been responsible for Clifton, Marsh and Pilling mills). Certainly the handmade brick incorporated in the current structure is identical to the bricks used for the many Derby estate dwellings and ancillary buildings still standing which also date from the early 1800s.

Yates' map of Lancashire dated 1796 shows forty working wind and water mills between the rivers Ribble and Lune including a windmill at Wharles. Kirkham, Treales and Clifton, windmills can still be seen from various vantage points in Treales. Of the mills remaining in the Fylde, Treales has the distinction, along with Lytham mill, of being built on a clay mound. There are possible reasons why this was done; to achieve additional height, drainage, or to protect the miller from the sweep of the sail. It could also be that in both cases the mounds had been part of the bases of earlier windmills.

Treales windmill is constructed on the Ordnance Survey 100ft contour, which is relatively elevated in the Fylde. It was strategically sited to catch whichever wind, but especially the South Westerly prevailing wind. If one stands on the eastern end of Kirkham railway station platform looking in the direction of Treales it is immediately obvious just how strategic that placing is. Treales windmill stands sentinel in the centre of a valley formed by Carr Hill on one side and Treales village on the other, a perfect landscape to funnel wind.

### Millers

The history of this building is inextricably linked with those who have performed the daily routines of milling on this site, drying, grinding, bagging, sail setting, braking, and maintaining the windmill in good order. We are fortunate in having been able to discover an unbroken line of miller/tenants to the time of the mill ceasing to work in 1928 and to the present date.

With the death of Henry Barnes the occupancy of the mill passed to his son, Richard Barnes. The 1842 census lists for Treales mill:

*Richard Barnes, miller, aged 45 years. Catherine, wife, aged 40 years, 1 son, 5 daughters*

It is assumed that Richard took over from Henry in 1822. The 1851 Census gives the same Richard Barnes but now describes him as *'Farmer of 90 acres'*, the role of miller then being in the hands of Richard Richardson, who had living with him at Treales his wife Ann, aged 42, born at Thistleton, and his daughter Mary, born at Treales. It is possible that the tenancy of the windmill was still held by Richard Barnes and that Richardson had been hired to work the windmill for him. It is known that the Richardsons moved to the water-mill at Bonds, Garstang soon after 1851. Whether Richard Barnes resumed the role of miller is open to speculation. He died at Treales in 1865 and is buried at the Willows Catholic Cemetery, Kirkham, but the tenancy of the mill had passed to Nicholas Cartmell between April 1851 and August 1853.

### The Cartmells

Nicholas Cartmell was born at Westby Mills in April 1814. He married Mary Barrow of Staining at Blackburn where he was employed as a miller. From 1840 until 1851 he was miller at Copster Green Mill, Salesbury, near Blackburn. The 1851 census taken at Mill Cottage, Salesbury, records that he had eight children between the ages of 15 years and 4 months. Three further children were born to him and his wife between 1851 and 1861 at Treales windmill confirming his move to Treales between 1851 and 1853. He was to be miller at Treales until his death on December 17th 1880, aged 66 years. He also is buried at the Willow Catholic Cemetery, Kirkham.

Nicholas was succeeded by his son Robert Cartmell who held the post until 1895 and from 1895 by Robert's son Bede who was to remain at Treales until he retired through ill health in 1902.

The Cartmells also had milling interests outside of Treales. It is known that Freckleton Water Mill (purchased from the Derby's in 1850 by the Cliftons), was sold again in 1882 when it became part of the endowment of a charity school (Newton Bluecoat). This mill was let to Robert Cartmell of Treales at £23 per annum on 11th February 1885 and again on the 16th February 1888 following a period when this mill was let to a Richard Pitt.

The same Robert Cartmell had two sons who worked in the trade with him, Bede, who took over the Mill at Treales, and Alban. Alban however was gifted as an artist and was sent to study in the artists' colony in Cornwall. He later emigrated to Canada where his artistic work is held in high regard. He was married from Treales Windmill in 1899. Bede's daughter, Elfrida, born at Treales 1897, gave us photographs of the working windmill and visited the mill until she was over ninety.

Henry Cartmell, son of Nicholas, born Salesbury 1851 but brought up at Treales Mill was miller at Marsh Mill, Thornton, where he died on the mill platform. Nicholas Cartmell, born Salesbury 1844 but lived at Treales Windmill later became miller at Newburgh Mill, Parbold, while Richard, Nicholas Cartmell's eldest son had a flour business in Fylde Road, Preston and was listed as miller of Cadley Mill, Preston, in 1871 census and a trade directory of 1861. A relative of the Treales family of Cartmell was miller at Dick's Mill, Carleton.

Following the turn of the century, many windmills were abandoned as other power was being developed for milling. However, following the Cartmell reign, the mill continued to work under two further millers, Mr. Bagot and Henry Hall until falling into disrepair from 1928. During this period the milling emphasis changed to mainly animal fodder production. Harry Hall (son) was born at Treales windmill when his father was the last miller to operate the mill. He now lives in retirement at Bolton Houses, the last village resident with a direct link to a milling tradition that has lasted at Treales from the early seventeen hundreds.

### Postcript

As will be seen from the illustrations, the windmill was in a state of decay as early as 1933 but was still to have its moment of drama. In 1938 the mill became tail-winded in a violent storm – the revolving cap mechanism failed to turn the sails into the wind, leaving the fan-tail facing the gale and the sails taking the full force of the wind on the lee side of the mill. The tower being in danger of collapse, the cap was removed by dynamite charge, the debris being blown into the surrounding field. Les Rawstrone, village resident, then aged nine, has vivid memories of being taken by his mother to witness the destruction of the cap and sails.

To maintain the tower and render the building serviceable as a storage unit, a lightweight conical cap of cedar shingle construction was manufactured by Rushton Brothers of Treales Yard in 1938. This enabled the mill to become a war-time storage depot for essential foodstuffs under the supervision of the mill's keeper, Jim Fisher of Windmill Farm.

Following the end of the Second World War the mill deteriorated. Its massive timbers were open to the elements, subject to rot and the ravages of those seeking to burn timber on house fires.

Nevertheless the structure merited listing as an historic monument (Grade II) and was therefore an embarrassment to the Church Commissioners (who had bought the Fylde Estate from the Derby Family) and who were legally obliged to keep the mill in good repair. In 1959 they sold the mill and mill ring to Shirley and Joe Lee who sought planning permission to convert the shell into a residence. This permission granted, conversion plans were drawn up by the Lytham architect, Tom Mellor, and

Estate workers at the Derby Bricks & Tile Works, Treales. This was situated opposite Sidings Farm, now the Boys' Brigade Headquarters.

conversion was undertaken by Marsden Rigby of the local building firm R.M. Rigby of Warton and completed on April 13th 1960. The 1928 lightweight cedar-shingle roof was badly damaged in 1987 by storms and Mr. & Mrs. Lee agreed with Fylde Borough Council to re-roof the structure with a traditional Fylde boat-shaped cap. This was constructed by millwright Joe Gillett of Wesham, and completed in November 1987. The new roof received a Conservation Award from Fylde Borough Council in 1989.

Treales windmill, its kiln and millers house has changed little since the tower-mill was first build in the early 1800s. It is still in a green lane as when visited by Allen Clark in the first quarter of the twentieth century. It is hoped these buildings, a unique part of the country's industrial heritage, will still be in good condition in 2099 and beyond.

## INDUSTRY IN THE PARISH
### Remembered by Les Rawstrone of Rawstrone & Hewitson, Treales Yard.

Les, who was born at Treales Laundry in 1929, has been associated with light industry and engineering for many years and as a 'native' is in an ideal position to put this important area of village life into perspective.
### Clay and Clothing

His first recollections were as a small boy, when with his friends, he often played in and around the Derby brick kilns and drying sheds at the Brick Works. These were situated opposite Railway Sidings (Boys Brigade Headquarters) on the outskirts of Treales on the road to Kirkham and produced the bricks and drainage tiles for the whole of the Fylde Estate. Of course his mother ran the 'laundry' which was situated by South View

maids, cooks, gardeners, as well as the laundry created by the Hale household and the Derby guests. There were no washing machines or spin dryers in those days; old fashioned boilers, rubbing boards and starch. However, he was quite certain that the days were sunny and warm enough to dry this large washing load naturally.

Les went on to describe the haberdashery and grocers shop kept by Mr. & Mrs. Shipley at Kington House, the second council house in Kirkham Road by the 'Derby Arms' and Roocroft's sweetshop opposite the Derby Arms. He insisted that this was never a Post Office, contrary to the belief of many who came later to live in the parish. The 'Derby Arms', then a small farm with at least six cows, also supported a cabin from which was sold sweets and ice cream.

### Busy Times

Light industry has been pursued since 1922 at Treales Yard when the Rushton brothers, Joe and Bill, built onto the existing Johnson's Treales smithy and began to cater for the needs of the farming community and for the Derby Estate. Both were joiners but Les remembered Bill Rushton as a master wheelwright who used the skills of Jack Johnson to manufacture iron banded cartwheels. There was always a need for farm carts and 'lorries' (the name usually given to four-wheeled horse drawn vehicles) wheel barrows, hen cabins, and later Dutch barns and stable and shippon fittings in wood and iron. This work was to expand on the declaration of world war II in 1939 when Rushton Brothers were given contracts by the Ministry of Agriculture to build barns and buildings for the increased agricultural out-put necessary to feed a population cut off from many of its

Farm providing a laundry service for Mowbreck Hall, the home of Lord Derby's agent, Mr. Hale and the temporary home of Lord Derby and his guests whenever they stayed in Treales for the hunting and shooting. Les remembered that the hounds for fox and hare hunting were kept at kennels to the south of the Brick Works in buildings that were later to be used for rearing pigs by the Johnsons. He remembered that the wash days were substantial ones as the staff of Mowbreck Hall was a large one. Butler, commonwealth food sources by German aggression. Another firm to benefit from war was Dick Hesketh's Garage in Treales Road. This became a Government-controlled depot for tractors and ploughs, servicing the grain and arable crop production throughout the Fylde. Les remembers two of the drivers, Archie Barr and Dick Porter, who later worked at the garage selling petrol. Further benefits accrued to Rushtons who now moved into the business of manufacturing motorised waggon bodies and removal vans, this work necessitating the erection of new buildings on land rented by Jack Johnson. The yard was now employing twelve men.

## Learning his Trade

Les left Kirkham Grammar School to start an apprenticeship with H.V. Burlingham of Blackpool as a panel beater and sheet metal worker, so it was little wonder that he gravitated towards the Johnson/Rushton yard in his spare time. Here he was given work repairing buckets, milking utensils and even helped shoeing horses. He also started to do car body repairs at home (Hill Cottage) much to the annoyance of several neighbours. By 1950 he was released from his apprenticeship as a fully qualified journeyman, but then had to do his National Service, serving in Germany for most of his two years, with the British Forces Broadcasting Service. On demobilisation he returned to Burlingham's, and then moved to Preston. to work on the Bond production line - Bond famous for the three-wheeled 'Bug' motor vehicle.

## Honest Toil

In the meanwhile Rushton Brothers had constructed a foundry, under the managership of a Mr. Parkinson, which made castings for Fylde Water Board - grid-tops, manhole covers, etc., even parts for Baxi fires. This enterprise accounted for the yard becoming known as 'Foundry Yard' to those who worked there. The foundry only prospered for a few years so Rushtons' diversified into pre-cast concrete products, manufacturing breeze blocks, lintels, cow boskins (stalls) and septic tanks. In 1956 Les rented accommodation from Rushtons' and started his car body repair shop and sheet metal works. When Mr. Hewitson joined him in partnership a new dimension emerged, spray brush painting and cellulose re-sprays. This increased their workload and they took on all Rushton Brothers painting.

When the Derby Estate was sold to the Church Commissioners, Rushtons and Johnsons bought all the land that they held for their light industrial use. Rawstrone and Hewitson expanded into larger units. By the mid-1970s Rushtons employed perhaps 45-50 craftsmen and labourers, Rawstrone & Hewitson between 10 and 14. Les considers that the demise of Rushtons, and to a large part, Rawstrone & Hewitson came about via the stringent regulations brought in by the Health & Safety Executive which would have required massive financial investment. Alan Rushton who was then running the yard closed it down in the late 1980s, converting the buildings into separate industrial units for lease. Clifford, Les's son bought the Hewitson share of their business and reduced their staff and building space, sub-letting to J. Giblin for car repairs, and Nuttalls for trailer hire and mechanical repairs. The yard now has many small businesses, Express Medicare Ltd., a national company with its Head Office in Oxford, David Greenhalgh, welding, servicing and supply of vehicles and light commercial vehicles, and a unit specialising in the building of horse boxes.

Les still has vivid memories of his youth when steam engines, steam rollers and steam tractors were a common sight on the village roads and of threshing machines which toured the local farms following the harvest. These were the vehicles owned and used by Isaac Ball & Sons Ltd., of Wharles. Les's enthusiasm for things mechanical is mirrored in his vintage vehicle collection with which he has spent much of his retirement and his pride in the Rawstrone ownership of 'Owd Isaac', perhaps the most famous of the Ball steam engines. This in its pristine form is often on show at Steam Rallies and Agricultural Shows. Treales boasts two other major contracting firms, both described by Les.

## Peter Marquis

Machinery bearing the name 'Pete Marquis' is a familiar sight on the parish roads and Peter claims to have worked for most parish residents at some time or another. Born and raised at Moss Farm, Salwick, which adjoins land next to Locking Stoops Cottage off Dagger Road, Peter was another casualty of the 'continuity' rules followed by Land Agents on behalf of their principals. His father lost the tenancy of Moss Farm and Peter and his siblings were forced to seek employment outside farming.

Initially he learned the many skills associated with contracting by working for Sandersons until he branched out to open his own business in 1991. He bought his first digger in 1992 and together with his two employees Billy and Harry, formed the nucleus of a company which now employs fourteen workers. Over the years, Peter's business has changed tack and moved towards civil engineering rather than its earlier agricultural base and he has worked on many prestigious schemes including the renovation of the sea coast defence at Blackpool, and the revamped St. George's Centre in Preston. Peter now tenders for work as far afield as Dumfries in Scotland. He is centred on Briars Farm, Lea.

## Sanderson of Moss Farm Lodge, Treales

The Sanderson agricultural contracting business was founded in 1950 by William James Sanderson. Born at Mee Farm in 1929 William was to work on the farm with his parents and brothers until deciding to commence his own business. Initially he purchased one tractor and offered his services to the community in a variety of agricultural skills. Married to Kathleen Swain, the family lived at Newton before purchasing Moss Farm Lodge from the Church Commissioners in 1968. Since then this family concern has been built up by the combined efforts of Mr & Mrs Sanderson and their children, Maureen (now Clark) William James (Junior) Christine, Irene (now Shuttleworth) and Andrew.

Early photograph of the *Eagle & Child*, Wharles, with a slate roof. It is now thatched.

### THE EAGLE AND CHILD

The parish boasts two public houses. *'The Derby Arms'* bears the crest of the Earl of Derby and therefore its name is self-explanatory, but how did our second hostelry get its name?

Sir Thomas Lathom of Lathom married the younger daughter of Sir Hamon Massey of Dunham Massey in 1343. After 12 years of marriage his only child was a daughter, Isabel, then aged 10. Sir Thomas was desperate for an heir and fell for the charms of a local girl; the daughter of a substantial neighbourhood yeoman named Oskatell. A son was subsequently born to the couple whom Sir Thomas was anxious to adopt to ensure perpetuation of his name. He assumed (no doubt correctly!) that his wife was highly unlikely to agree to the adoption of his child and

the infringement of their own daughter's rights. Sir Thomas, and a loyal trusty servant, in whom he had confided, hatched a plot.

A message was conveyed to the baby's mother to have him ready for a servant to take him to the hall the next morning, she being strictly forbidden to follow. She readily consented to this, assuming Lady de Lathom had agreed to raise the boy and joyful at the child's enhanced prospects. The servant, however, transported the baby in his wicker cradle to the foot of a precipice close to the place where he and Sir Thomas knew a pair of eagles had nested. The servant then concealed himself in a nearby thicket.

Meanwhile, Sir Thomas and his lady were embarking on their usual morning stroll although they ventured further afield that day. In a shady

Rearing chickens the old way, Phyllis and Keith Shipley at Ivy Cottage, Treales.

Harold, Jack and Nellie Cookson.

Church View Farm, Treales.

dell, not far from the eyrie, Sir Thomas suddenly stood still and listened, his lady also tensed and listened. The short and feeble cry of a baby was heard and Sir Thomas sprang forward feigning astonishment at the discovery of a child which had evidently been dropped from the talons of an eagle. The child was jointly viewed as a special gift from Providence, taken home, nursed and baptised Oskatell. Lady de Lathom became very attached to the foundling believing his adoption was dictated by the will of Heaven. Sir Thomas readily agreed! To give greater credence to this supposed miracle and to remove suspicion of fraud from prying eyes, Sir Thomas assumed for his crest an eagle on the wing, proper, looking round as though for something he had lost.

In the twilight of his years, Sir Thomas began to reconsider his wrongdoings. His daughter, Isabel, now the widow, Lady Stanley, received her just inheritance. Sir Oskatell of Lathom (who was knighted by King Edward) was not left entirely destitute. To him and his descendants were reserved the manors of Irlam and Urmston (near Manchester) with other valuable inheritances. At the same time he was given the signet of his arms 'an eagle regardant, proper'. It was only subsequent to the supplanting of Sir Oskatell that his rival took the present crest 'The Eagle and Child' where the eagle is represented as having secured his prey in token of their triumph over the foundling, whom he is preparing to devour. The crest, with the motto SANS CHANGER, the descendants of Sir John Stanley, the present Earls of Derby continue to hold.

The 'Eagle & Child' at Wharles, a most interesting hostelry with a long history is currently in the hands of Brian and Angela Tatham.

## SOME VILLAGE CHARACTERS

### George and Robert Barnes

This father and son team are an essential element in the economy of the village. Always 'open' at Wharles Smithy, and with their mobile workshop they are able to keep the farming community working when disaster occurs to machinery at inopportune times. Nothing seems to upset the equilibrium of this team; no job is too difficult. Theirs is a life of dedication to the community. Their skill and ingenuity, be it fabricating machinery parts, fathoming the intricacies of hydraulics or differential gearing is legendary. Tucked away in a quiet lane, Wharles Smithy is perhaps the most important hub of our village life.

### Adrian Birch

A villager only by adoption, Adrian has served us as our most regular postman as long as most of us can remember; his familiar figure and post van are an everyday essential part of our lives. Never ruffled, always

a smile or a cheery wave we have been grateful to him in so many ways for his help, kindness, sociability, his care of the lonely and elderly on his daily round, and for his friendship.

### Mrs. Blackburn

She was always to be seen, even in old age, riding though the village on a bicycle with racing handlebars, dressed in a long dark coat and matching cloche hat, clutching a capacious handbag. Her husband was the gravedigger at Treales Church and his choice was always to dig graves at night-time, his wife holding a lantern for him while he worked. In her later years she fell downstairs at her home, Rock Cottage. True to character, although both her wrists had been fractured in the fall, she rode her cycle to Kirkham to obtain medical assistance

### Stephen Cairns

Stephen Cairns of Derby Farmhouse, Treales, is perhaps better known to the parish as the Consultant Physician at the Royal Preston Acute Hospital. His voluntary ministrations to parishioners who have been suddenly taken ill or who have had long term debility has not gone unnoticed by the community. Many will be grateful to him for his kindness and care beyond his professional hospital role.

### Hetty & Edith Crane

Born and bred at South View Cottage in Treales, Hetty (Ethel, b.1886, d.1971) and Edith (b.1883, d.1969) lived the whole of their long lives without benefit of bathroom or running hot water. Theirs was a life of self-sufficiency with enough land ('croft') to support hens, a cow, and for the production of vegetables for their needs.

They were famous for their 'poke' sun bonnets which they both wore, both village characters in their own right. When Hetty died (she outlived Edith by a short time) her bedroom was a collector's treasure trove. At the foot of the half-tester bed was a large dome-lidded wooden trunk containing periodicals, books and other printed materials from the early Victorian Period. Under the mattress on the same bed was found a loaded revolver of the type issued during the American Civil War.

When Edith was in her early eighties, she unfortunately fractured her hip in a fall and was hospitalised at Preston Infirmary. Tenacious to life, she recovered and returned to South View well, if still slightly immobile. However, she failed to make the medical improvement that was expected and her doctor could find no reason for her relapsed condition. Questioning Hetty, (who was looking after Edith) one day, the doctor discovered that as well as the prescription medicines, Hetty had been giving Edith a daily dose of salt and water. *"Whatever have you been giving her salt and water for?"*, he asked incredulously. *"Well"*, came Hetty's sure reply *"salt and water preserves your body after death"*. Without the home remedy Edith made a quick recovery.

Note: New woodland planted in 1993 adjacent to South View Cottage has been named 'Cranes Wood' for Ordnance Survey purposes; a mark of recognition for the family who lived there for most of the twentieth century.

## Derek Emmens

Derek, initially from Manchester and a former Guardsman, came to Treales with his family in the late sixties. Since that time he has worked at Grange Farm. Now aged 64 he has always been interested in athletics and road-running and took up the marathon as a sport in middle life. He has since raised a considerable amount of money for various charities through sponsorship. He is perhaps proudest that he has won a London Marathon Medal for each of his six children, among the many medals he has gained for running. He successfully completed the London Marathon 2000 in April.

## Mrs. Emery

A devout Christian, she was one of the kindest and most genuine of women. Nothing was too much trouble for her and she was a very great asset to the village during the many years she lived at Hill House with her husband Cyril, with whom she raised three adopted children. Both she and Cyril found great joy in attending Christ Church, Treales.

## 'Jem' Fisher

Jem who had the smallholding known as Windmill Farm worked this property throughout the Second World War when the then disused Treales Windmill was used as a store for essential foodstuffs. In the small one acre orchard in front of his house he was able to make his annual rent by growing just two crops, daffodils and onions, both of which he sold on Preston Market. He was a frugal man and wasted nothing. According to legend when his daughter was married one Saturday morning at Treales Church, Jem retrieved the wedding bouquets, dismantled them and sold the flowers on his market stall in the afternoon.

## Katie Hall

Katie's boast is that she is the only foreigner living in the parish holding a British passport. She came to Treales at the end of the Second World War as the young bride of Harry Hall who had met and proposed marriage to her in her native Malta when Harry was serving in the Royal Navy. We are glad that she came.

## Heinrich Hart

Heinrich, a prisoner-of-war from the German Army was captured in the later years of the Second World War, interned, and later worked as a farm labourer in Treales. He never returned to his native Germany. A large, extremely strong man, who never properly mastered the English language, he was nevertheless a true countryman and had a deep affection for and uncanny empathy with both wild and tame beasts. He, his wife and children, Robert, Sally and Suzie lived at one time at Windmill Cottage and later in retirement at Clifton.

## James Hogarth

James was a farmer at Moss House Farm and for many years served on the Parish Council. He also served on the Fylde Rural Council and was Chairman of the housing committee. In recognition of his services to the community Hogarth Crescent at Wharles was named after him.

## Ann & Tom Ogle

They arrived in Treales in the mid-sixties, a middle aged couple from Tipperary in Southern Ireland where Tom had worked for the Countess of Rosse. They had accepted a job at Garlicks, Moorfield Farm.

Their only luggage was a large and badly scuffed cheap suitcase and two old fashioned sit-up-and-beg bicycles. In their deep Irish Brogue they marvelled at what were unfamiliar sights to them – the Ribble double-decker buses. *"Just like they have in Dublin"*, and *"the cars going by all the day"* along Treales Road. A delightful, sober and upright couple and devout Roman Catholics, they were to be seen in their 'Sunday best' cycling to Mass in Kirkham on Sabbath and Saints' days. Always unhurried and serene Ann was the epitome of my vision of a saint.

While Tom farmed, Ann found cleaning work in Kirkham and at the Derby Arms where she worked with Bella Rossall. Theirs is a sad tale however. Farm amalgamation led to Tom's early redundancy and unable to find permanent employment they were left with little option than to return to Ireland. They departed as they had come - with the same two bicycles and a battered suitcase, their dreams of a better life shattered. Within months Ann was dead. Of a broken heart?

## Jack Parkinson

A diminutive, cherubic figure usually to be seen wearing a flat-cap, blue boiler suit and wellies, he lived and farmed in Treales throughout his life working first with his father, and later in partnership with his sister, Grace, and brother-in-law, Robert Baxter. His face always shone as if it had been polished and he spoke in an excited, staccato manner, once heard never forgotten. He knew all his cows by name and to see them run to him whenever he entered their field was a revelation. They loved him.

## Mike & Sean Peters

Following in the footsteps of the legendary Dick Hesketh, but almost a century later, the village has a father and son team who excel at the dangerous sport of motor racing. A lifelong follower of the MG marque,

Mike in his early forties has encouraged his son Sean, eighteen, to follow him into joining the MG Car Club and to race for one of the oldest motor sport trophies, the Cockshoot Cup, given in 1933. While Sean still has to race in the MG Standard Class, Mike races in the more competitive senior section. 'Standard' means that the car as raced is little changed from the MG Midget road car, only strengthened in terms of safety structures and increase braking potential. The 'Senior' car, however, which develops 150 b.h.p. is a stripped out version, fitted with sealed fuel tanks, roll bar, racing seats, full racing harness, modified steering, suspension, and brakes. To complete the modification it is fitted with slick racing tyres and automatic fire extinguishers.

Mike has recorded four outright wins; at Brands Hatch, Silverstone and Oulton Park, all in 1999. He was third in the overall championships in 1997 but bettered this in 1998 when he finished second. Mike once found an abandoned MG in a lake in America and had it shipped back to England for restoration. He has recently given a restored MG A to the British Heritage Museum in Warwickshire. Mike is the Managing Director of Universal Products of Greenhalgh, nr. Kirkham.

### Rawstrones

The Rawstrones lived in a half-timbered house close to the Derby Arms. Mr. Rawstrone was an Inspector for the Ribble Bus Company; a tall, smart and distinguished figure in his immaculate uniform. Mrs Rawstrone was for many years the Secretary of the local branch of the Women's Institute. Their son Leslie Rawstrone, founder of Rawstrone & Hewitson has worked (and continues to do so in retirement) in the village for most of his life. He makes the daily journey from Kirkham to restore old vehicles to their former glory. He perhaps more than most has contributed more to this 'history' of the village. Les and his wife Irene have an extensive memory, which, together with their collection of archive material related to the village have added much to what is set down within these pages.

### Tom & Bella Rossall

Tom and Bella lived in Rock Cottage for many years, each with a distinct claim to being a *'local character'*. Tom had an enviable job, lengthsman, keeping the road between his home and Carr Hill in Kirkham. With bicycle, brush and shovel he passed the time of day with everyone he met along the way. Their large garden was immaculately kept, their hens, vegetables and soft and top fruit helping greatly to their self-sufficiency. Their marriage was long and often tempestuous; they seemed to need the chemistry associated with a difference of opinion to cement their close relationship. As so often happens in such dependent marriages,

when Bella died, Tom, lost without her, lasted only a very short time. They both died in 1999.

### Heather Speak

In this Millennium year Heather, of Rose Cottage, Wharles, is the Chairman of the Treales, Wharles and Roseacre Parish Council and is the representative member for the ward on the Fylde Borough Council. She has become a champion of the parish in many ways, fighting tirelessly against the proposed Motorway Service Station planning application and is currently engaged in promoting a better ambience for the village by spearheading 'Fylde in Bloom'. In the short while she has been in office she has made a dynamic impact on matters relating to the whole community.

### Frank & Phyllis Walker

Following the Second World War the garden at Middleton Cottage contained one of the most superb displays of bedding gardening to be seen anywhere in Lancashire. That this was so was to the credit of Frank and Phyllis whose seed-raising prowess, pricking out and patient planting resulted in this annual masterpiece of controlled colour and design. Not that this talent ended with bedding. With two greenhouses, Frank and Phyllis raised *Coleus* plants that were the wonder of the country, and for many years the major prizes for *Coleus* at the Southport Flower Show found their way back to the sideboard at Middleton Cottage. Sadly the partnership foundered with Phyllis's untimely death but there are many in the village who will recall this annual miracle with the greatest pleasure. Frank will be interested to learn that the taxonomists now call Coleus - *Solenostemon*.

### Harold Wynn

Harold and his wife Ann made their home in Treales when Harold was appointed to the post of Surveyor for the Church Commissioners in the late 1960s. He is a most talented man, as dextrous at taking apart and re-assembling motor car engines as he is at repairing antique clocks, a skill he learned in his formative years when he was responsible for the winding and maintenance of all the clocks in a famous Midlands stately home. When the Church Commissioners sold the estate in 1971 the Wynns' moved south, Harold becoming a Surveyor with Cheshire County Council. They now live in retirement near Chester.

### Charlotte & Sally Speak and Lucy Barnes

These young pupils of Treales School have followed in a well founded tradition for charitable works in the parish by organising and raising considerable funds for the Blue Peter Appeal for premature babies. That their Blue Peter Bring & Buy Sale should have raised over £150 for the care of babies born in need of true life support, should make us all realise what good there is around us and the selflessness of the young if nurtured in the right traditions.

## Equestrian

At Moss House Farm all the Gardner children are keen equestrians. They regularly enter competitions and have all had some success in 1999. Sally aged 6 came first in the leading rein at both the Garstang Show and the Goosnargh and Longridge Show.

Fiona age 9 came third at the Royal Lancashire Show in the Equitation Class and second in the North West Championship Working Hunter class.

Edward age 11 was second in the Lancashire points in the British Show Pony society Working Hunter class and first in the Westmorland County Working Hunter class.

## Football

One of our local boys, Andrew Robinson of Cross Hill Farm, plays for Kirkham under 16s. In 1999 the team had quite a successful season. They were the proud winners of the Hogan Cup final which was played at Bloomfield Road. He was also named clubman of the year in 1998.

## Rugby

Wayne Rayner, aged 18, is a keen rugby player and has played for Preston Grasshoppers and Lancashire as well as Lancashire clubs. The highlight of his career so far was a 22 day tour of South Africa in 1999 with his school. They played six games and travelled the length of South Africa.

## Hockey

We have several talented hockey players in the parish including Victoria Peters and Ellie Cairns who are both 16. Victoria represented Lancashire in the under 16s hockey championships during 1999. Ellie is also a member of the Lancashire under 16 hockey squad and holds a regular place in the first team. Victoria also excels on the athletics field, representing Lancashire in the 100 meters in 1998 and becoming the under 16s Lancashire schools long jump champion in 1999.

Leanne Sharples at the age of 13 is also a keen hockey player. In 1999 she captained the Lancashire under 13 squad and in 2000 she captained the under 14 squad. In 1999 she was accepted for the under 16s Northern Development Group, quite an achievement for a 13 year old. Leanne's sister, Becky, seems to be following in Leanne's footsteps by playing for her schools' under 11's team.

✧✳✧✳✧✳✧

## ISAAC BALL OF WHARLES 1859 - 1943

Isaac Ball became a legend in his own lifetime, but when the parish was canvassed for information on this pioneer of steam in agriculture, very little was forthcoming. His empire has now disappeared. 'Balls Yard' is now covered with a small housing estate. It was rewarding therefore to speak to Les Rawstrone who informed me that the Rawstrones, (who married into the Ball family) were still the proud possessors of 'Owd Isaac' one of the famous steam engines which once graced Wharles and which, like many others, has been lovingly restored, and is to be seen frequently at Steam Rallies throughout the country.

Les also pointed towards another source of information on the Ball family, an article written many years ago for 'Steam Magazine' by Arnold Staples and Alan Porter, both steam enthusiasts. Porter has compiled a list of all the steam engines thought to have been owned by the Ball family, and has managed to trace those that were not broken up.

### On Foot and Ferry

Isaac Ball was the eldest son of John Ball, farmer and thrashing contractor from Banks, Nr. Southport. He worked for his father during the 1870s but wishing to start his own business, walked from Banks to Freckleton with his wife. Part of this journey would be by ferry from Hesketh Bank across the Ribble, and following a period when he worked on a farm in Freckleton he moved to Wharles where he started his threshing business in 1881. To do this he had purchased a second-hand Marshall steam-driven threshing machine, but the site at Wharles allowed him space to build workshops and a yard area which would later accommodate his fleet of engines.

### In Tandem then Solo

For a short period between 1890 and 1893 he joined forces with his brother John, who was living at Winmarleigh, Nr. Garstang, and the firm became known as I. & J. Ball. This was a period of expansion and in 1890 the brothers ordered a new 8 h.p. s.c. (single cylinder) Marshall to be quickly followed by a new 7 h.p. Burrell and two more 8 h.p. s.c. Marshalls.

John decided to set up his own business at Forton and took with him the 1892 Marshall Engine (No. 21049) which Isaac replaced with a new Marshall (No. 23885) which was built to his own specification having a short wheelbase. Delivered in 1894 this was the last Marshall engine to be purchased by the Balls as by then Isaac had become friendly with Charles Burrell of Thetford in Lincolnshire, Steam Engineer, who was to become a frequent visitor to Wharles.

In the early 1900s Isaac became an agent for the sale of Burrell engines with the result that his business increased dramatically. Not only could he

The first convertible engine No. 2626 was presented in 1903 and this was followed by a further six during the next 10 years, and by the outbreak of Word War I in 1914 he had at least ten engines and threshing sets and seven road rollers, which were mainly employed as contract machines to local authorities, especially Lancashire County Council. During the war the fleet increased further by two second hand machines. Others followed in the 1920s there being considerable business to be had in the Fylde. Indeed, 'his' area stretched from Ribble to Wyre, his western boundary being the A6. His brother, who had also expanded his business, serviced the area north of the Wyre and land to the east of the A6. In terms of road-rolling there were no boundaries to be recognised and it is believed that Isaac's road rollers went as far afield as Barrow in Furness and east as far as Bacup.

### Technology Harnessed

It is often forgotten in these days of the mobile phone and world - wide web that in earlier days communications between customer and contractor were slow and difficult, almost as slow as the pace of the steam engines themselves. However, Staples and Porter researched that the Balls were often ahead of their rivals in this area. Should an offer of work come while the engines were working elsewhere Mrs Ball would telegraph the information from Kirkham Post Office (the nearest to Wharles) to the Post Office nearest to where the engine was working. Isaac would call then at this Post Office at the end of a working day and make an instant decision to divert his machines to the new customer. This saved many miles and hours of travel.

His second strategy was to distribute postcards (advertising Burrell products) to clients in order that they could post their wishes to Wharles. Mail was a quick method of communication in the first half of the twentieth century, most communities receiving two deliveries per day. His third innovative method was to provide his daughter, who worked for the firm, with a pony and trap. Using this method of transport, messages could be taken to Isaac on site, baling wire delivered to the threshing 'sets', and money collected from debtors to the company. By 1914 though, the telephone had arrived at Wharles and the other methods became largely redundant. About this time Isaac himself became an administrator and travelled around the countryside

now afford to increase his own fleet, but could take on the repair and rebuilding of Burrell engines in the North. He had, however, a perennial problem, that of idle machinery once the thrashing season was finished, and with Burrell's help he overcame this by suggesting that a *convertible* engine could be built – from traction engine to road roller. With this idea implemented, Isaac was firmly established as the main Burrell agent in Lancashire, and continued to be until the collapse of the Burrell firm in the early 1930s. He was to sell many engines to contractors, local authorities and travelling showmen. It is known that he had a very impressive stand at the Royal Lancashire Show of 1902, which coincided, with the Preston Guild celebrations of that year.

supervising his enterprise by motor car, initially by De Dion Bouton and following the war by a Model 'T' Ford.

## More Strings to Their Bow

During the First World War the firm also became agents for binder twine and local farmers were pleased to buy from the Ball Yard rather than make the long journey into Preston. The local term for this twine became 'Owd Isaac'.

As threshing and rolling business increased so did the repair work and the variety of work in the yard multiplied. The range of machinery at Wharles was extensive and it was now possible to do complete rebuilds of engines on site. Such renovations as re-boilering, replacing the fire boxes, re-tyring the wheels and re-boring cylinders were common everyday tasks. During 1930-31 engines were stored at local farms because of lack of space at Ball's Yard.

## Time Marches On

By the onset of World Ward II the running of the business was in the hands of Tom, Isaac's youngest son, but it is said that no major decision was taken by anyone other than Isaac until his death in 1943, at the age of 84 years. The firm did receive a setback in the late 1930s when a fire destroyed many threshing sets and the overhead crane used for lifting heavy items. However, repairs were quickly made which was probably as well, the yard becoming even busier during the war. At this time it was estimated that fifteen threshing sets were in action employing eighty men, and with twenty rollers at work the repair shop was always kept at full stretch. The firm employed so many men that they were able to field both a football and cricket team of their own. The war was to bring military work for the firm; steam rollers being employed in the construction of air strips at Samlesbury and Inskip, and road ways for the camps at Weeton and Inskip, in addition to the regular work for Lancashire County Council.

The heyday of the firm, however, had passed and decline was inevitable with the advent of the tractor and combined harvester. Another blow was to affect the yard when Lancashire County Council employed its own road rollers in 1946 and a lucrative contract was lost. Tom Ball still concentrated his efforts on the road rolling business but inevitably the agricultural work diminished. In the 1950s there were a series of disastrous fires in the Fylde, and Ball's Yard was the scene of such a conflagration in 1956. Many threshing machines and engines were lost, together with specialised tools for repair work, the total damage estimated at £18,000.

William, Isaac's eldest son went to work with his uncle at Forton and eventually took over the business.

Peter, the second son was appointed to Charles Burrell at Thetford, eventually becoming foreman of that business. He was personally responsible for the building of many engines; in particular a revolutionary spring-mounted three-speed machine in 1911. He returned to work with Isaac at Wharles soon after 1911 but then moved to be engineer for Lancashire County Council.

Tom, Isaac's third son, born in 1889 was apprenticed to Vulcan Motors, Crossens, Near Southport. He returned to Wharles and eventually took over the firm on the death of his father. It is to Tom Ball that the steam enthusiasts owe the survival of so many of the Ball engines. He was adamant that none of his engines should be scrapped, a fate which lay in store for all the John Ball engines at Forton. Tom Ball's two sons, John and Victor continued in the family business as did David, John's son.

## THE DERBY LEGACY

It is written elsewhere in the text regarding the paternalistic role of the Derby family towards those living and working on the estate. John Melling described the dubious practice of farm amalgamation by the Church Commissioners when there was no male heir to continue with the farm. This, as we know, caused much distress to many widows and their families whose livelihood was curtailed at very short notice. This contrasted markedly with George Barnes' recollection of an estate of small farm holdings where tenants could learn their trade and be moved on to larger farms when they had proved their farming worth. Grace Baxter told of her father working for the Derbys in another capacity before being offered South View Farm. There is evidence also that in the days when the Derbys held the estate that women were not only allowed to remain on their farms following the death of their husbands but were given tenancies

in their own right. This it would seem was as enlightened a policy as might be found anywhere in the country.

Other evidence of the generosity of the Derby family has come to light in the memorabilia passed to the Millenium Committee, some of which is worthy of mention here. The earliest, dated 1924, was contained in a letter from Windham Hall, the Derby Estate Manager, and sent from the Estate Office in Preston to all those working in the parish for Lord Derby. In the letter Hall explains that he has received the following instruction from Lord Derby following his lordship's success in the classic horse race named after his family:

*'I am anxious that everybody in my employ should have something with which to buy if they wish a small souvenir of SANSOVINO'S victory and therefore I want you to pay to everybody an extra week's wage.'*

When, in 1948, the Earl of Derby married Isabel, the daughter of Mrs Milles-Lade at Westminster Abbey on Thursday 22nd July, the tenants of the Derby Estate received invitations to the wedding.

However, not only did they receive the invitation to the wedding but additional information regarding their welfare on the journey to London. On the invitation it had been stated that *'arrangements will be made to convey all who accept to and from London'*, and subsequently they received details of those arrangements. Guests, the 'Fylde Party', were instructed to leave their cars on the site of 'Burnt-out Mill, opposite Kirkham Goods Yard' before joining the special London train which left Kirkham Station well before eight a.m. Each received a programme setting out the meals which would be served to them during the day:

| 8am | on train | bacon rolls & tea |
| 10.30am | on train | Ham rolls, cheese & biscuits, fruit cake, beers & minerals |
| 4.00pm | Savoy Hotel | refreshments |
| 6.30pm | on train | Sausage rolls, corned beef rolls, cheese & biscuits, tea (if possible), beer & minerals |

No doubt a good time was had by all.

Another interesting document came from relatives of the late Christopher Swan and was dated November 16th 1948. This was received by Swan from the solicitors, Lawrence, Graham & Co., 6 New Square, Lincoln's Inn, London, WC 2 regarding the will of the seventeenth Earl of Derby. It describes the terms of the will in respect of legacies to be paid to those who had been employed by the Earl at the time of his death. The amount of the legacy to be received was calculated as follows:

*The Seventeenth Earl of Derby deceased*

By his will the late Earl of Derby bequeathed to each of his servants employed by him, and who did not receive salary or wages in excess of £500 per annum [excluding: a) any servant to whom a separate legacy was bequeathed. b) any servant under notice to leave and c) any servant who should at his death have been in service less than five years) a legacy of one month's wages or salary in respect of every five years of continuous employment with him… From information furnished by the Executors you appear to be entitled to a legacy of £159.5.0. calculated as follows:

| Amount of wages per month | No. of 5 year periods | Amount of legacy |
|---|---|---|
| £22.15.0 | 7 | £159.5.0 |

*A cheque for this sum is enclosed herewith and you are requested to sign and return the attached form of receipt, stamped and dated.*

*Lawrence Graham & Co.*
*For the Exors. of the late 17th Earl of Derby*

To an employee earning a weekly wage of little over £5, this was a very generous legacy indeed.

### POSTSCRIPT

From the evidence of the previous pages the parish of Treales, Wharles and Roseacre, has been in continuous change for most of its existence. It has evolved to what it is today through periods of war, pestilence, poverty and prosperity. The number of farms has decreased as different farming methods have industrialised the countryside. Its population has varied with family size and employment opportunities, but in essence it has changed little in that it has remained a rural entity; an oasis of green sandwiched between the ever increasing conurbations of Preston and Blackpool. It must always have been an area of natural beauty which we would do well to preserve.

That demands will be made on our parish is still evident. In 1999 the community fought hard, united perhaps as never before in its history, to overturn a planning application to develop a large section of parish farmland into a Motorway Service Station. The parish members protested, not because the proposal was 'in our own backyard' but because such a development was totally unnecessary and would have duplicated services which already existed nearby.

Similarly there are those who wish to quadruple the parish housing stock by opposing the agreed permitted Fylde Borough Council development boundaries for the parish. This too has been opposed and rejected, if only temporarily.

But not all is doom and gloom. Indeed, one feels a new spirit of community beginning to evolve – a true desire to evaluate what is good in the parish, and to improve the ambience for the general good.

The village school, its children our hope for the future, is a thriving and enthusiastic centre of educational excellence well supported by the community and 'Friends'. The curriculum introduces the young to cyberspace but also reminds them of their roots in the earth that most will tend as they go though life. The school maintains its close links with the church which, although now sharing a vicar with Christ Church, Wesham, still holds a central position in the social and spiritual life of the community.

A new optimism has been signalled from our Parish Council which is embracing the modern era by becoming more interactive with the community by discussing its deliberations in an overt and positive way. The council's initiative to involve the parish with Fylde in Bloom (first in Treales but next year extended to Wharles and Roseacre) has resulted in a dramatic change to the village ambience. Flowers now burgeon from tubs, hanging baskets and stone-troughs planted and maintained by volunteers from all sections of the community.

The *Derby Arms* has been sold into the private sector by its former multi-national brewery owner and in its newly renovated form is likely to cater well for locals and visitors in its proposed new guise as 'a good place to eat'.

Changes have occurred also in our highways and bye-ways. A new tradition of letting hedges grow taller as shelter for farm stock and habitat and food source for wildlife is gathering momentum and this Millennium year has seen an unprecedented show of sloe and hawthorn blossom adorning our countryside. Another welcome trend is to allow sapling trees to grow in the hedgerows, forming avenues along many of our country lanes. One of our farming families is leading an experiment in association with the Highways Department of Lancashire County Council, to leave its verges uncut to encourage the re-establishment of wildflowers. This is an initiative which if successful could be extended to every verge in the parish. Already a solid core of volunteer parishioners is raising seedlings to reintroduce once common native wildflowers, harebells, bluebells, cowslips, primroses, wild roses and honeysuckle into our byeways. Avenues of trees have also been planted in this Millennium year and plans are being made to plant screen-trees to hide the less pleasant sightlines of the parish.

The Parish Council have also indicated that they wish to save 'heritage' buildings within the parish from demolition, and have moved to influence the type of dwelling that will be built in the future as part of the permitted development, wishing to see a more vernacular design more in keeping with existing older dwellings.

Most in the parish would agree that Treales, Wharles and Roseacre form a unique rural paradise within the Fylde. Most would also agree that the parish should remain rural - a place of tradition, work, and recreation, which will retain its unscathed identity throughout the next Millennium. It will only remain so by the continued vigilance of the village.

ARMS : *Argent*, on a bend, *azure*, three bucks' heads, cabossed, *or*.

CREST : On a chapeau, *gules*, turned up, *ermine*, an eagle, wings endorsed, *or*, preying on an infant in its cradle, proper, swaddled, *gules*, banded of the third.

SUPPORTERS : Dexter, a griffin ; sinister, a buck ; both *or*, and ducally collared and chained, *azure*, the buck attired of the last.

MOTTO : SANS CHANGER.

### Acknowledgements

Special thanks must go to all those people in the parish who have helped in the production of these recollections and who are not mentioned by family name in the text, Pauline Coxon, Marjorie & Stan Swift, Mrs. Sandra Wright (History of Treales School), Christine Manton, Les Green, Jose Pearson and Paddy Astley (Cartmell family of Millers), Joan Trippier (Gamekeeping), Christine Howarth, Alan & Mary Stephenson, Meg Hancock, David Webster, Brian Rawstrone, Ian Porter (Isaac Ball), Karen Baugh, and Cath Huggett, who without complaint has typed and retyped the manuscript several times. The committee is deeply indebted to Cath for the time that she has devoted to this unenviable task. Thanks also to all those who have provided interesting photographs and printed material.

## Residents of Treales, 2000 (Alphabetical Order)

Gill Armer
Jane Armer
Thomas Armer
Charlotte Armitage
Gillian Armitage
John Armitage
Sam Armitage
Debra Bates
Lucy Bates
Sam Bates
Stephen Bates
Jonathan Baugh
Karen Baugh
Sam Baugh
Grace Baxter
Jan Beasant
Sara Beasant
Chris Benson
John Benson
Lily Benson
Rhona Binks
Steve Binks
Hilary Blair
John Blair
Carol Bradshaw
William Bradshaw
Alan Burrows
Dawn Burrows
Gertie Burrows
Joshua Burrows
Thomas Burrows
Alastair Cairns
Andrew Cairns
Eleanor Cairns
Mary Ellen Cairns
Steve Cairns
Jennifer Cartwright
Malcolm Cartwright
Andrew Christie

Margaret Clark
Alan Clowes
Harry Compson
Margaret Compson
Daniel Cook
Frank Cook
Jean Cook
Rebecca Cook
Gillian Cookson
Lucy Cookson
Olivia Cookson
Stephen Cookson
Eleanor Cooper
Jimmy Cooper
Jennifer Counsell
Michael Counsell
Michael Coxon
Pauline Coxon
Christine Cross
Dave Cross
Michael Davies
Erminio Delcurto
Marjorie Densley
Paul Densley
Colin Eccles
Sylvia Eccles
John Egan
Sue Egan
Melanie Ellis
Derek Emmens
Edna Emmens
Andrew Ferguson
Rosemary Ferguson
Mark Fieldhouse
Martin Fieldhouse
Wendy Fieldhouse
Barry Fitzgerald
Claire Fitzgerald
Emma Fitzgerald

Edward Gardner
Fiona Gardner
Jilly Gardner
John Gardner
Sally Gardner
Jeff Goodier
Mary Goodier
Lionel Gowland
Liz Grove
Ruth Grove
Sarah Grove
Steve Grove
Liz Haines
Martin Haines
Megan Haines
Nick Haines
Robert Haines
Avril Hale
Harry Hall
Katie Hall
Hannah Hardman
Julie Hardman
Mark Hardman
Matthew Hardman
Thomas Hardman
Trevor Hardman
Alison Harwood
Frederick Harwood
Sammuel Higarth
Chloe Hind
Sally Hind
Samantha Hind
Vernon Hind
Colin Hogarth
Janet Hogarth
May Hogarth
Samuel Hogarth
Caroline Holtappel
Natalie Holtappel

Nathan Holtappel
Cath Huggett
Kate Huggett
Ralph Huggett
John Isles
Jean Jamieson
James Johnson
Joan Johnson
Katie Johnson
Lynn Johnson
Thomas Johnson
Tom Johnson
Caroline Kay
Greg Kay
Nicholas Kendrick
Pat Kendrick
Roger Kendrick
Sarah Kendrick
Daniel Kidd
Linda Kidd
Matthew Kidd
Gemma Leach
Jade Leach
Sandie Leach
Steve Leach
Joe Lee
Shirley Lee
Alan Lennard
Essie Lennard
Christine Manton
Peter Manton
Wendy Manton
Derek Matthews
Sheila Matthews
Bob McAlpine
James McAlpine
Niall McAlpine
Ross McAlpine
Genevieve Melling

Gwen Melling
Helen Melling
James Melling
Oliver Melling
Marion Morgan
Roly Morgan
Dennis Morley
Isabel Morley
John Morley
Susan Morley
Ian Murdoch
Lorna Murdoch
Max Murdoch
Andrew Myerscough
Jack Myerscough
Edna Orr
Harry Orr
Alan Park
Alan Parker
Marjorie Parker
Maureen Parker
Nicholas Parker
Robert Parker
Heidi Parkinson
Henry Parkinson
Martin Parkinson
Adam Partington
Luke Partington
Maria Partington
Mark Partington
Olivia Partington
Mike Peters
Paul Peters
Sean Peters
Stella Peters
Victoria Peters
Francis Price
Jacqueline Price
Laura Price

Damian Rayner
Sue Rayner
Wayne Rayner
Emily Reynolds
Jane Reynolds
Jessica Reynolds
John Reynolds
Michael Reynolds
Karen Rickson
Peter Rickson
William Rickson
Yvonne Rigby
Elaine Roberts
Lucinda Roberts
Martin Roberts
Martina Roberts
Andrew Robinson
Bill Robinson
Brian Robinson
Jennifer Robinson
Lena Robinson
Mark Robinson
Matthew Robinson
Bill Salisbury
Kath Salisbury
Alan Sanderson
Bill Sanderson
Caroline Sanderson
Cath Sanderson
Christine Sanderson
Rachael Sanderson
Sue Sanderson
Barbara Sharples
David Sharples
Geoff Sharples
Gillian Sharples
Ian Sharples
Jessica Sharples
Leanne Sharples

Rebecca Sharples  
Sarah Sharples  
Hannah Smith  
Jackie Smith  
Keeley Smith  
Keith Smith  
Linda Smith  
Linden Smith  
Mike Smith  
Andrew Southwood  
Lise Southwood  
Thomas Southwood  
Marjorie Swift  
Stan Swift  
Marie Taylor  
Rowland Taylor  
Joan Trippier  
Alan Walker  
Frank Walker  
Mary Walker  
Rebecca Walker  
David Webster  
Charlotte Welch  
Janina Welch  
John Welch  
Stan Wood  

## Residents of Wharles, 2000

John Atherton  
Carolyn Bamber  
Jane Barnes  
Lucinda Barnes  
Robert Barnes  
Howard Burrows  
Pat Burrows  
Anne Butcher  
Bob Butcher  
Daniel Butcher  
Trish Butcher  
George Carter  
Jean Carter  
Robert Carter  
Colin Caulfield  
Suzanne Caulfield  
Janet Chedd  
Melissa Chedd  
Rebecca Chedd  
Jim Coleman  
June Coleman  
Thomas Cowell  
Darren Ellis  
Louise Ellis  
Lesley Fare  
Lyndsay Fare  
Phillipa Fare  
Stephen Fare  
Gordon Foster  
John Fry  
Margaret Fry  
Ann Gilfoyle  
Mary Gillett  
Graham Gunn  
Pearl Gunn  
Alan Hall  
Albert Hall  
Andrew Hall  
David Hall  
Dorothy Hall  
Eileen Hall  
Esther Hall  
Helen Hall  
Matthew Hall  
Nancy Hall  
Pam Hall  
Simon Hall  
Paul Heseltine  
Rosemary Heseltine  
Jack Hull  
Kevin Hull  
Linda Hull  
Sam Hull  
Barbara Hurton  
Roger Hurton  
Lesley Longton  
Janet Meredith  
Jean Molloy  
Margaret Molloy  
Michael Molloy  
Sian Morris  
James Nisbet  
Annette Parkinson  
Lorraine Parkinson  
Spencer Parkinson  
Poppy Price  
Tim Price  
Ann Prince  
Carl Prince  
Naomi Rawcliffe  
Shaun Rawcliffe  
Alice Richardson  
Alice Richardson Foster  
Matthew Richardson Foster  
Helen Salisbury  
Flo Slack  
John Slack  
Charlotte Speak  
Frank Speak  
Fred Speak  
Heather Speak  
Sally Speak  
Sam Speak  
Bethan Stafford  
Joyce Stuart  
Robert Stuart  
Susan Swift  
James Swiift  
Angela Tatham  
Brian Tatham  
Barbara Tolson  
Ian Tolson  
James Tolson  
David Utley  
Oliver Utley  
Trisha Uttley  
Frank Walsh  
Pat Walsh  
David Wild  

## Residents of Roseacre, 2000

Alex Beaumont  
Conrad Beaumont  
James Beaumont  
Yvonne Beaumont  
Paul Bentley  
Susan Bentley  
David Brock  
Nichola Brock  
Jean Cunningham  
Ian Daniel  
Linda Daniel  
Ben Davies  
Daniel Davies  
Pamela Davies  
Paul Davies  
Colin Davis  
June Davis  
Julie Evans  
Michael Fare  
Pat Fare  
Peter Fare  
Robert Fare  
Ruth Fare  
Paul Gardner  
Susan Greaves  
Philip Harrison  
Susan Harrison  
Andrew Hills  
Robert Hills  
David Jackson  
Kathryn Jackson  
Lynne Jackson  
David Knight  
Valerie Knight  
Ann Leftley  
George Leftley  
Gary Monaghan  
Gillian Monaghan  
Chris Noad  
Christine Noad  
Nicholas Nutter  
Christine Pickervance  
Harrison Pickervance  
Harry Pickervance  
Julie Pickervance  
Sonya Pickervance  
Thomas Pickervance  
Victoria Pickervance  
Christopher Roberts  
Janet Roberts  
Judith Roberts  
Peter Roberts  
Betty Sanderson  
Bob Sanderson  
Christine Stuart  
Darren Stuart  
Lyndsay Stuart  
Jackie Sylvester  
Jim Sylvester  
Matthew Sylvester  
Andrew Thornley  
Annie Thornley  
Grace Thornley  
Jim Thornley  
Rachel Thornley  
Marshall Towers  
Richard Towers  
Kath Waldron  
Barry Warner  
Elizabeth Warner  
Neil Williamson  
Elsie Yates  
Mary Yates  
Richard Yates  
Robin Yates  
William Yates